A MERE MORTAL

Enjoy!

Mal x

£8-99

A MERE MORTAL

I pay my bills on time but there must be more to life

Mal Harris

INTRODUCTION

They say that everyone has a book in them. I don't know whether this is true, but not everyone sits down to go through the process, so most potential books remain unwritten. Which means that some writers are creating more than their fair share to judge by the proliferation of paperbacks in the world.

Why add one more to the millions of tomes out there already? Especially a biography.

To be fair, I have read hundreds of biographies and autobiographies about the good, the bad and the downright ugly, though majorly, people I admire or find fascinating.

I have thoroughly enjoyed reading about Frank Sinatra, Elvis, John F. and Jackie Kennedy, and a fascinating assessment of Wallis Simpson.

Books about Jackie Stewart, Geoff Hurst, Bobby Charlton and Bobby Moore have been read cover to cover.

I have delighted at biographies vis-à-vis Bob Dylan, John Lennon and Olivia Newton-John, and thrilled at accounts of Noel Coward, Michael Palin and Marilyn Monroe.

I have smiled my way through books by and about Eric Sykes, Hancock, James Corden, Brian Blessed and Rob Brydon.

It does not make me an expert by any means, but what I find enthralling about all of these characters is their journey from relative obscurity to fame. That journey and the paths they took, either deliberately or knowingly in the case of a Bowie, or a Dylan, or purely by accident or a chance meeting, such as that when a young Lennon attracted the attention of Beatles' manager Brian Epstein.

Then, at the other end of the spectrum, there's me, and my short journey around the block!

Would anyone want to read about someone who never achieved fame or notoriety? What would make them fascinating enough to engage the reader? What would make **me** find it interesting to read about me? I mean I have had more than my fair share of interesting encounters, and could tell you about some of my near-misses, but other than that?

What would be my driver? What would I hope for my reader to get out of the experience?

Just for a moment, let's look at my motivation for writing.

I wonder whether you are like me?

Do you sometimes look at someone at work, or listen to somebody perhaps on the phone or in the media, and think to yourself, 'who on earth made the decision to employ them, who took *them* on'?

It might be a radio presenter who struggles to complete two sentences without hesitating over a word or a pronunciation? Maybe a newsreader who fluffs his or her lines? Otherwise, maybe a television presenter who is fine with a script but who is totally out of their depth without a cue-card, stuck for what to say or how to respond.

Then, there are the telephone contact centres, where your adviser just fails to listen to your problem, and attempts to 'solve' your issue by reading mechanically from an answer template, from which they are seemingly unable to deviate. If your particular problem is not one of the common ones listed in front of them, they persist in continuing to ask arbitrary questions from their script, until you simply give up and put down the phone.

Sportsmen (or women for that matter) who fail dismally on the day, maybe through lack of effort; bank officials who offer poor advice; actors, particularly on television, who are walking, talking, planks of wood, and, as the saying goes, couldn't act their way out of a paper bag; workmen who make a botched job in your house and have to call back to repair it, or haven't got the part and have to order it from the warehouse, or worse, from abroad.

Then there are the politicians who always fail to answer a straight question on Question Time, or who renege on manifesto promises; drivers who cut you up on your trip to work or fail to let you in at those busy junctions, when it must surely be obvious to them that you are late or in a hurry.

I have always been hyper-critical of people I come across in all walks of life. I pick up on speech impediments, poor use of grammar, untidy looks, lack of professionalism, body odour, failure to understand an issue at first time of asking, hesitation, lack of intelligence or, worse, stupidity, sheer incompetence: you name it and I will tend to criticise, to the point where my wife becomes weary of it, and, I have to say, of me too, and not without reason. "Will you leave that poor man alone!"

When the person in question is already successful in another field of activity, I become even more disapproving, if that's possible. What do I mean?

I have little doubt my favourite example would be one of the many former excellent and gifted footballers-turned- pundit, with their 'the boy done good', 'the manager fetched him on too soon' and 'we was all getting excited'.

On the other side of the coin, this is not to say that there aren't celebrities who excel in more than one arena.

Examples are manifold. Comedians generally make superb actors, think of Billy Connelly, Robin Williams, Whoopi Goldberg, who all started out as a stand-up, or Lenny Henry for that matter.

Many sportsmen and women take to presenting on television and radio like fish to water, think of the now much improved Gary Lineker, athletics commentator Steve Cram and former tennis star Sue Barker. They have the looks, the knowledge and the skills to pull it off.

Singers such as Justin Timberlake branch out into other fields with equal success. Singer Cher, rapper Marky Mark, now remarketed as Mark Wahlberg and chanteuse Jennifer Lopez have appeared in hugely successful movies.

And just about anyone in the public eye can hold a tune or even star in a musical – think of Philip Schofield for one, or maybe Kate Winslett or Catherine Zeta Jones, whose singing talents were not perhaps immediately obvious.

Politicians can dance, well, sort of.

Actors, and sportsmen, and comics, and presenters, and politicians, and singers too, it seems, write children's books.

And, having thought about the concept for many years, so did I.

Maybe I thought that, with the story having come to me so easily, with it seeming so natural and so pure, that everybody would love it as much as I did. How could anyone not like a funny adventure story about a little blond curly-haired girl and three magical animal friends, written in simple language and uncluttered by modern-day apparatus such as mobile phones and computers?

MAL HARRIS

The big difference for me, was that it appeared so very easy for someone already in the public eye to get their work published. Hardly a day went by without hearing some actor, comedian, sportsman or singer pushing their latest children's book. Not only did they get published, but in many cases their books flew off the shelves, where mine languished on some agent's dusty backroom cabinet, or worse, in the bin.

Admittedly, I did receive many nice letters, all congratulating me on the sweetness of my story, the delightfulness of my characters and the excellence of the illustrations. For each of these compliments however, there was a gentle dismissal. The book didn't quite fit in with the agency's current agenda or the book (as lovely as it was) didn't suit its readership. They all mentioned the vast number of books they received, while almost all referred me to the Writers' and Artists' Yearbook, where I would find helpful hints and tips, and the addresses of other agencies and publishers.

The question I asked myself then was, where did they think I had got their address from in the first place if not from that book? Hadn't I followed all the suggestions in the writers' 'bible' anyway?

This book, therefore, provisionally entitled 'The Average Man', or 'The Nearly Man', was going to start with a rant against the famous.

Take someone like the wonderful Sir Chris Hoy, whom I totally admire as a brilliant world-beating cyclist. I marvel at his fitness, his speed and his single-minded attitude to bike racing. I even enjoy his co-presenting, which is insightful and entertaining.

My argument though, was going to be 'What chance would I have as a writer of a children's story compared with Sir Chris, who has written his story of the little boy with a bike?' Given the choice of marketing a book by Sir Chris with his background, and a children's picture book by an ex-council benefits employee, which do you think an agent or publisher would pick? And of course, I know the answer.

However, until my wife quite properly asked me the question, I never considered that my efforts may just have been all so much garbage, whereas Chris for his part had a natural talent for writing. If my book was so stunningly brilliant, she suggested, surely it would have stood out from the rest, like a beacon on a misty day at the coast?

For goodness sake, I knew already that agents took on no more than a handful of new writers each year from the many thousands of scripts they received. It took someone close to me to open my eyes to the truth, that mine simply was not good or appealing enough.

It might be interesting to have a look at how such a book might have started:

Let me start by asking you a question; have you ever been extraordinary at something, anything? You know, EXCEPTIONAL at something, an expert? A one off? A genius?

If you have, it is probably not the only thing you are good at is it, because people who are brilliant at one thing tend, on the whole, to be annoyingly good at most things.

Or, at least if they are not, they have the agents to get them publicity sufficient to make their mark.

Pretty scathing.

But, you know, since I first put pen to paper, my views have changed, and fairly radically to boot. I will come to the reasons for my change of heart in a little while. Fair to say however, that the book's course has taken a diversion.

And now for the erudite bit!

The psychology of dreaming of success is perhaps explained as follows:

On a conscious level, at one point or another, all of us think about both what has happened, and what might have been. Like me, you might wonder what your life would have been like if you'd followed your heart and married your college sweetheart, or decided to take that apprenticeship instead of going to university, or maybe taken that lower-paid job with the greater prospects. What if you had decided to take that job on a cruise ship and travelled the world? Who would you have met? Who knows how things might have turned out?

The fancy name for this "If only" thinking is 'counterfactual thinking'. I believe that it plays an important and complicated role in how we human beings make sense of all of our experiences—both good and bad. How we use 'if only' thinking, says a lot about who we are, and whether we are able to sustain happiness and cope with setbacks. But we cannot live life like this, to the exclusion of the real world. Living permanently in a world of 'if only' may result in disappointment or even depression.

Are we all guilty of counterfactual thinking from time to time? I know I am.

So, where should I begin? I know, traditionally it has to be at the beginning. But it's not quite that simple. The beginning of what? My life? Possibly, but then this isn't your run-of-the-mill straightforward autobiography, you know; parents, born, school, university high jinks, exciting career, more and more success, glory, awards, retirement, an appropriate life for an autobiography like those I have already enjoyed reading.

Me? My perception is that I am 'average'. Always have been. Maybe, if one is being generous, just a shade above average. At most things. Not everything. But most things. If I am in a group of 10, I would normally finish 3rd or 4th but rarely last, occasionally first. I can turn my hand to quite a few different tasks and do them reasonably well without excelling. Yet, having said that, I still believe myself to be merely average. Fifth or sixth out of ten? That is how I see myself, but am I right? Am I doing myself a disservice?

When I left university, I regularly, and for many years, received an alumni newsletter, for former students. It was satisfying to read about exciting projects at the campus and it reminded me of 3 happy years in South Wales. At the same time, I was depressed by the articles written by 'successful alumni'. Over the months I grew tired of chief executive officers, managing directors and chairmen all smiling out at me from the shiny pages of the magazine. They listed their achievements, their promotions on the steady rungs of success. I know it was out of jealousy, and I just longed for something in my life to crow about.

What I was evidently forgetting was that by being top at junior school, mid-form in the top class at grammar school, and with a 2 (ii) degree I was already pretty special, in perhaps the top 2% of the country. Surely this should have been enough?

Yet I retained this feeling of being average? After all, to continue the theme, a '2 (ii)' is the average degree obtained by UK students.

With this in mind, I began my book. I was intent on demonstrating to those who cared to read it, how unfair the world of publishing is. To me it appeared that almost anyone famous (or, for that matter, infamous) could write almost anything, and purely because of their celebrity status be certain their work would be published. I ignored, for the moment anyway, my self-perception of averageness. If I had stopped to ponder for a second, that assessment alone would have provided me with the 'why' my picture book had not been snapped up by at least one of the publishers I had contacted.

As I wrote, it dawned on me gradually, that at particular moments in my life, I had decent enough opportunities to make something of myself, in spite of my apparent limitations.

Once, while I was preparing content for a website, I listed out the jobs or serious hobbies I had been involved in over the years, and it went something like: teacher, lecturer, auditor, bank employee, radio presenter, insurance clerk, stock-broking office worker, hotel entertainer and host, singer, supermarket worker, writer, deejay, actor, benefit office clerk, tribunal presenter, photographer and sports shop salesman. Not an inconsiderable number or range of activities. Not so bad for your average man!

Maybe, that is where I should begin, with my ordinariness, my perceived 'averageness'.

Nothing wrong with being just average of course.

Joke alert! My Maths teacher called me average. How mean!

I probably do myself an injustice too, because it is not the fact that I fail to reach excellence in any one area of expertise, but rather my failure to take advantage of opportunities that have come my way to propel myself down the road to comparative success. Most people have one chance in life to realize their ambitions, and a mere few grasp the nettle and go on to accomplish their goals.

I am lucky. I feel that I have been at the crossroads so many times it has become almost embarrassing. There have always been rivals, doubts or excuses at crucial moments, and it is these that have served to shape my success or failure. Sometimes I have felt confident in my own ability, sufficient to take on the world, but more often than not, fear or indecisiveness has prevented me from taking up the cudgel and fighting my corner.

There have been several moments where I have been at the 'crossroads of life' and had awkward decisions to make. Moments of what I like to call 'almost-ness', not one of those words that the spellcheck seems to like. I sometimes ponder over whether there is a link between 'average' and 'almost', the two big 'A's: after all, if you discover that you are only modestly talented at something for which you have real ambitions, the more unlikely you will be to succeed, or at the very least your journey will be made that much more difficult.

I appear to have had more than my fair share of almost-ness, instances of 'sliding doors' where my career or sometimes just my life could have progressed in a totally different direction.

This marks a change in my interpretation of Mal Harris, as a person, and therefore the course my book must take. No longer will I rail at the world of publishing, blaming all but myself. My change of heart results from a realisation that my interpretation that I am in truth 'average' may well be correct, and that in life we achieve no more than we are each capable of. I did in the end get my children's book, 'Shubby and the Mammacs, The Golden Crown', published, even if it was through a self-publishing company at minimal cost. I sold a few to friends and family. I pitched up at fetes and galas and was delighted to sell 5 or 6 per day, enjoying the sunshine and the occasional chat about Shubby and her origins.

So, Mal, what happened and what could have happened? All those what-ifs. I will attempt to set it all out before you. Make up your own mind.

The people I have encountered, the Lord Coes, the England rugby youth 'probables' I went to school with, the international footballers I knew and met, the celebrity singers and actors I have interviewed, the famous athletes and top sportsmen I have been involved with, my close encounters with careers in the media and the theatre, my early promise and my later uncertainties.

Remember, as we start this journey together, that most of my trickiest decisions have been informed by my belief that I am just average.

After all, I am a mere mortal.

1. A FAR FROM AVERAGE BEGINNING: CHILD GENIUS?

Come on, that has got to be some exaggeration? Really? A child genius? Weren't you just saying you were average, and now you were almost a child genius?

It had all started so very well. My parents kept a little record book to show my progress, first tooth, first steps, weight then, weight now, and to believe my parents I spoke my first words at 8 months, which, if true, would be spectacularly early, particularly for a lad. Records show that I uttered those immortal words 'dad' and 'bab', but these are open to interpretation of course. Noises that sound random to you and me suddenly become fully formed words to the imaginative parent.

I can't claim to have walked early but, courtesy of my father, I did have a ball at my feet almost before I could put one foot in front of the other.

Moving to Gloucestershire at the tender age of four, I had started school at my local primary in Churchdown aged 4 and a half. No reception class in those days. No pre-school or nursery. Anything you learned before school had to be from your parents, or siblings, and as an only child, with dad in the forces and often away either abroad or in the workshop, my mother was my chief source of information and my constant carer and companion. Whereas dad had gone to his nearby grammar school and showed much potential, mum had attended the local secondary school. She had passed exams but only at the piano, and yet she never struck me as lacking in intelligence. She had a wonderful memory, and was always an enormous help with testing my spelling, for someone who, as she put it, only went to 'elementary'.

Perhaps surprisingly, in the light of that, from day 1 at primary school I showed amazing promise. In my first year I received a year-end prize of a book about a cat and a goldfish, for 'outstanding work', and for the next 6 years, year on year, I was the recipient of book prizes for 'Excellent work', 'Outstanding year', or, as soon as we were tested, 'First in Class'. I have them all, boxed and somewhere in the attic, one about the Heroes of Greek Mythology, another, great ships from history, another, Scientific Marvels of our time, which latterly, 55 years on, makes interesting reading in view of recent developments.

My mother always said that I could read the newspaper before I started school, and clearly the teachers were very impressed with my efforts. I seem to remember Miss Trotter in year one saying that, in her experience, she had never seen anything like it.

In real terms, what it meant was that, by the time we made the transition from infant to junior school, at the end of each lesson, I had finished my work way before the others. Even the quick and consistent little Irish lad

Earl struggled to keep up with me, though admittedly he was occasionally quicker at maths. I sometimes idled my way through the last 10 minutes of a lesson, rarely pushing myself to find extra topics to read. In fact, in the last two years of junior school the teachers became so accustomed to my early finishes that they took advantage of me to hand out the free milk and orange juice quotas, to my own class at first, then around the rest of the school.

Usually it would be me and A.N.Other racing to the milk area, class numbers in hand, to count out the required bottles into a crate, and to whisk the crate off to the appropriate classroom, knocking and entering before the break-time bell.

All this in spite of an horrendous attendance record!

My school reports show a child who was never late for school, but in one year I was absent 124 times. I am not sure how many people would be aware that absences were recorded in those days in half days, nonetheless it does mean that little Mal missed 62 days through illness.

For sure I don't recall every sick day I had to take, but I do remember being absent with something like measles for several weeks only to catch scarlet fever and be off immediately for several weeks more. I was a sickly child. I had a nasty bout of croup as a four-year-old. I caught German measles and chickenpox, and constantly suffered from colds and sore throats.

Back in those days when you were off, you caught up immediately on your return by borrowing note books from your friends and copying their work, including drawings and cut-outs. You also caught up on stories and 'compositions', your inventive essays. End of year tests dictated your position in class, and I was intense and keen to do well. Looking back, I suppose I had more time to revise. I could spend hour upon hour sat in my sick bed catching up and memorising. I was blessed with the kind of silly memory that once I had read something a couple of times it stuck. I find that even now I find myself remembering telephone numbers read out to me if it needs redialling half an hour later. Handy too when you come to write an autobiography!

I was also so lucky to have the sort of parents who were desperate to assist by buying English and Maths self-help books. These books featured test after test of basic English and Maths. The English books included grammar and punctuation tests, spelling and comprehension exams while the maths books tested addition, multiplication and long division. These tests were timed, and dad gave me no injury time allowances or time-out at the watering hole. I took pleasure and delight at hitting 90% plus, and I have little doubt that this discipline aided my progress at junior school immensely.

It might be hard to imagine such overwhelming dominance these days, but back in the 1960s we learned from books, and books alone. Those who read a lot and could retain the information and then regurgitate it at exam time did best. Somehow, and seemingly without too much effort, I managed to come top every year from year one throughout to year 6. Trotter, Nelmes, Walters, Scott, Gregson and Davis, six teachers whose names I have remembered to this day, all signed my brilliant yearly reports in glowing terms.

I was supreme at English in spite of my Welsh background, my spelling was immaculate, my reading more advanced than my years. In year 6 my reading age was over 13 and the word I struggled with in the test was 'miscellaneous', that 'c' being mysteriously silent it would appear. My maths was excellent, in particular mental arithmetic. You could throw anything from the times-table at me. My IQ test results staggered the teaching staff, and though I couldn't draw for toffee, I could copy and trace. And my writing was neat and tidy. In short, I had all the constituent parts to be a remarkable pupil. Top for 6 years, was I the first genius that my school had produced?

Can you imagine the effect this had on both me and my parents, who took the comments the teachers made as gospel? From their point of view, I could do no wrong, at school in any case. For six years _they_ believed my press. I must admit that I was taken in by it too. It had all come too easy to me. I began to coast along in the knowledge that I was special.

In year 6, or top class as we knew it, Mr Davis regularly asked me to help out the weaker members of class, going from desk to desk to assist them with their problems. Names such as Barbara and Lavinia ring a bell, but there were half a dozen or so kids who struggled to keep up, and I was there for them, while Mr Davis stayed in his accustomed spot behind his desk at the front of the room.

Teachers relying on me to help out in class? Surely, I must be some sort of prodigy?

So, from the point of view of my education I guess you could say I was doing all I needed to do to succeed. Was there anything I was not capable of?

However, all this early success had the effect of setting me up for a fall.

And perhaps this is where the story should have begun.

You would seriously question at that stage any intentions I may have had to write a book about being average, of being a 'nearly man', and yet, even at this tender age, the signs were there if one had looked carefully.

Graham Marshall and Alan Taylor were to blame, though to be entirely fair to them it wasn't their fault. Come on Mal, how can that be? Explain yourself, please, you say.

I was a fast runner as a child, and my father had given me a ball to play with at a very early age. The combination of these two factors led me to be a super quick sprinter and a reasonable football player. I always ran to school from the age of 4. It wasn't far round the block and then one road to cross and I was there in the entrance to school. I could do it in one go, and as I got older, the quicker I made it to school. I was slim and wiry with powerful leg muscles, inherited from dad.

I used to come home for lunch too, so got extra practice, pretending to be the UK sprint champion of the day, Peter Radford. The only real test of my speed against lads of my own age would come annually on sports day.

Step forward Graham Marshall. He was taller than me, but then most kids were. I was only average height.

I do not recall how far the straight sprint was. Our school playground was smallish and the other side of the toilet block was an area of grass which stretched the length of the playground and the headmaster's block, maybe 80 yards (70 metres), so although it felt like we were doing the 100 yards, just like my heroes, it was probably more like 70 yards, and over the rough grassy course marked out with chalk into lanes specially for the event.

There was regularly a big rivalry between Graham and me. I don't remember winning in the years up to year 6 when I would have my final chance to beat him – Graham was to fail his 11 plus, though he was later given a second chance to progress to 'grammar'. I don't think we had much to do with each other apart from our sprinting rivalry.

I was nervous. I always seemed to be nervous to be honest. That pent-up anxiety that I felt most days in the effort to finish my work first and escape to the milk and orange delivery.

I was nervous at the start line just as I had been in class one morning when the teacher asked us all about what had gone on the previous day at afternoon break-time. It seems as if a gang of boys had made one of the girls cry. She had run into the headmaster's room in tears.

I remember it as clear as day. I even remember her name, but common-sense and decency dictate that I keep that to myself. One or two of the lads liked to tease this girl, who was not the brightest, nor if I am honest, one of the prettiest. They liked to push and shove her to the point where they would hold her down on the grass and lift her skirt.

On this particular afternoon it had gone too far. One of the boys tried to pull down her knickers while the rest of us stood around, either sniggering or like me just keeping out of the way. We did nothing to intervene. These days we would have been held just as culpable. In spite of this I recall the feelings of guilt by association as the headmaster addressed us all and tore us off a strip (no pun intended).

Back at sports day there was no escape however, and the gun went off. I stumbled out of my imaginary blocks and was already behind. My pick up was smooth and I was soon sprinting, getting closer to the giant alongside me. Being the best student was OK but it wasn't the same as being sporting best. Sportsmen were popular, I was just clever. I wanted to be popular too.

I was catching up fast, but the ground was not even beneath my feet. Once again, I stumbled. There were just yards to go. With a big effort I was certain I could be first to the tape – it was probably just a string of rope –

and I went for it. I dipped for the line, but deep down I knew that however close I felt it was, and there were only inches in it, I had been beaten by the better man.

I was more likely to pass my 11 plus I had to tell myself. Was this any consolation?

Second in the race would still not be good enough. Graham was surrounded by his team-mates. He was 'the man'.

Dad was a decent footballer, hockey player, rugby player, you name it. He even played rugby for Cheltenham, and, before that, for occasional Welsh champions, Newbridge, on his leave from the Fleet Air Arm. So, I had a great coach in the sporting field.

I also had a wall on the road front against which I could practise my football, and, over the road, a grassy island on which a football pitch could be marked out with jumpers for goalposts. The road surrounding the island made an excellent racetrack for running and cycling, so as well as being my personal gym, the island also allowed me to practise my footballing skills.

My uncle Roy was also a decent enough footballer and he was the one who taught me to control the ball, strike a 'banana shot' and how to keep my head over the ball and not to lean back when shooting at goal.

At junior school we played football all the time when we weren't playing kiss chase. I loved playing kiss chase, mainly because as one of the quickest runners I could snare any girl I took a fancy to. There was only one girl for me, and I usually caught her in the cul-de-sac between classes 2 and 3 but then merely stood there with her to protect her from other predators. I did get a friendly peck from this delightful young girl and it was recognised that we were an item, me and Sandria Nelson, the only Sandria I ever met, just as my mother was the only Malrie.

Break time football then, because as you know I ran home for lunch. And I was fairly good at it all, passing, dribbling, tackling and running with the ball. Not as good a winger as Brian Lennox, whose feint to put in a cross 'had' me every time, sending me the wrong way as he glided past me, the ball stuck like glue to his boots.

Nor as silky skilled as Robert Base, who was my favourite player in class. Rob's problem was, that he had suffered badly from an attack of meningitis, and as a result was supposed not to play sports, not that it ever stopped him. But overall, I was just about the best all round footballer. That is, until the arrival of super Alan Taylor.

Alan moved into our area towards the end of junior school, in Mr Gregson's class, from a place I had not heard of, Billingham, and he had this strange accent, a bit like Welsh. Turns out he was a Geordie. And not only a good-looking lad, but, dammit, funny and sporty. In fact, the perfect mix as far as popularity was concerned, and it spanned both sexes.

I continued to be top of the class. Only Christine Davey challenged my superiority and only in English lessons. I could write a smashing story, but if we were asked for a two-page story that is precisely what they got. Many a time a story ended abruptly at the bottom of page two with "and they all went home for tea" or some such phrase. I usually got high marks for originality and of course for grammar and spelling, but often with a comment to the effect that my story had come to a sudden ending, or that perhaps I could have made the tale a little more complicated or expanded on my theme. Chris was more inventive than me and had built-in stamina when it came to composition.

In year 6, Alan came into his own. We had a football team, of sorts. Rob was able to play nothing more than a bit part. Brian played on the wing, but we were a small school with only 15 or so lads to choose from. And that meant that anyone who could tackle had to play at the back. In spite of my eye for goal, keeping my head over the ball and striking that banana shot, I qualified for full back courtesy of my ability to tackle.

Alan was a striker, one of the best I had ever seen, a natural, skilful on both flanks, and he could head the ball. Balls in those days were made of steel or so it seemed. Or concrete, but bloody hard whatever. Alan was the only one brave or stupid enough to plant his head on these balls. Our defenders certainly didn't, or wouldn't, and one particular lad used to spectacularly duck out of the way to preserve life and limb.

We played in all weathers. One Saturday morning found us shivering at the local secondary modern, where we had to play having no pitch of our own, heavy frost on the ground and sleet blowing in our eyes. We played the full match in gloves. A couple of lads had jumpers on. We lost. At half time it was going that badly they put me in goal, me, the only one that could tackle! That ploy didn't help, because without me to intercept, the opposition simply had even more shots on target. We sank, and the ground conditions were the only thing preventing us sinking further.

We set a record that year. We went without a win. Our best away performance on a sloping pitch was a reasonable 13-0 defeat.

Despite all these humiliations Mr Davis was asked to recommend boys to take part in the Gloucester Schools under-11 trials. He automatically picked Alan Taylor, and much to my surprise, young Malcolm. I was going to be a footballer just like my cousin Trevor.

Actually, Trevor was strictly my dad's cousin, being his uncle Alb's son. But when you find a link with a well-known footballer at the age of 11 you tend to fabricate as close a tie as you can. And there was no doubt that Trevor was not only a promising player but a lovely fellow to boot.

Trevor Hockey started out as a ball playing winger at Bradford City, and while he had also been a promising rugby league player just as his father had been before him, he attracted great interest from the top clubs such as Tottenham Hotspur, before moving to Nottingham Forest and going on to Newcastle United where I saw him first pitched against the might of Cardiff City's international star centre-half, the giant John Charles, at Ninian Park.

Dad and I travelled to Cardiff on the Newcastle train with the players, meeting Trevor on the platform at Gloucester. Trevor showed us the bruises up and down his legs sustained in playing as a winger. He admitted that he could put a mean tackle in himself, but most of his bruises had been the result of cowardly kicks when the referee's back was turned.

I also sat in the main stand at St Andrews, watching Trev play in midfield for Birmingham City. They came from behind at half-time to beat Wolves 3-2, and after the match we were ushered into the club committee room bar to meet the team. I was just a little bit in awe of Barry Bridges, the Blues' number 9, and among the non-playing guests that day was boxing heavyweight Johnny Prescott who had beaten the 'Blond Bomber' Billy Walker over 10 rounds in London. Both dad and I checked our fingers after shaking his giant hand.

Trevor went on to play for Wales, by virtue of his grandfather, and cropped up again in my life at the strangest of moments more than once. I watched from the stands as he played against Finland at Ninian Park in Cardiff. It was a cold October night in 1971 and the game was a Euro '72 qualifying match which Wales won 3-0.

The morning after the Wales game I walked into Cardiff, and called at the Wales team's hotel right in the centre of town and waited in the lobby as instructed. Through the doors at the far end of the lobby came the players one by one, including Peter Rodrigues who I recognised as another Sheffield based footballer with 'Wednesday'. Ironically, at the time, another of the team's fullbacks was Rod Thomas who had attended my grammar school and played for Swindon Town.

Another great occasion took place in my university town of Swansea. A testimonial match was arranged for Len Allchurch, a Welshman who had played extensively for the Sheffield United, so it was appropriate that Swansea's opposition should come from United. It was an opportunity for me to see Trevor play with some of United's greatest. Hodgkinson, the goalkeeper, had recently announced his retirement. Up front two of my favourites were playing, Gil Reece and Alan Woodward, while Trevor sat in front of the back four to provide a platform for another of the game's greats, Tony Currie, an England international goalscoring midfielder.

After the eight-goal match, won by Sheff U 5-3, Trevor met me in the away changing room. He was fresh out of the showers, and excitedly introduced me to the team. His best mate, Colin Addison, had accepted a role as manager to Hereford United, and he was suited and booted. Trev had asked his team-mates to sign my programme, and they had left enough room for him to sign it 'to my cousin Malcolm'. Then came the moment I will never forget, nor stop bragging about in football circles.

Trevor asked whether I had met Tony Currie. I struggled to stammer, 'No'. "Come on then!" he said, and promptly walked me over to the communal bath where Tony Currie was splashing around with another half a dozen players, his long fair hair plastered to his face, mud everywhere, on what had been a damp night. "Tony! My cousin Malc!" said Trevor. And without further ado I shook the soppy hand of the mighty blade. "Pleased to meet you!" I stuttered. "Likewise" said the golden one.

Meanwhile, on the brink of my own footballing fame and notoriety, a date came through for the trials. Teams were published, and there I was in the same team as Al, now my pal Al, my team-mate.

How could I not like him? Everyone liked him, didn't they? And as if to supply proof of the fact and to yet again demote me to my rightful place in life, a vote was due to take place. I am not sure that in these politically correct days it would even be contemplated, but back in the late sixties it did not appear out of place to run popularity contests, and in top class we were asked to select our favourite boy and girl in class. Of course, this directly pitched me against super Alan, quick-as-lightening Graham, and speedy winger Brian, who infamously had had the temerity to fight me in my own back garden over my girlfriend Sandria Nelson.

I was not the best looking of children, but I had fair hair and a winning smile. I could tell a tale. My use of English was exemplary. I could run and I could play football. Plus, I was bright and intelligent. How could I fail to be popular with others?! I was kind too, thought the best of everyone and tried not to upset others, so when the vote came, I was confident but not expectant.

Who won? Well, first of all, did it bother me who won? I so wanted to be popular, more than anything, so naturally I wanted to win. Being first in class had long come easy to me.

There were only 30 votes to play for. 29 I suppose, as sadly I could not vote for myself. Would that one vote have made any difference? Who won? Just a minute, I know you are desperate to know now. I realised that I was up against it. I rallied the troops. Sandria had left the area and moved away, and I was missing her. One less vote to count upon. I still had a few friends I knew I could count on.

When we arrived in Churchdown from Wales I had a really strong Welsh accent. A sing-song accent that differed extensively from the local Cotswolds accent and marked me out as a target for fun, and much, much more. Pushing, shoving and bashing, and insults to the extent that from an early stage I decided to ditch the accent of my birth by copying the presenters on the Light Programme, the forerunner of Radio 2. Friends became that much easier to find with an English accent. Maria and Jennifer always seemed to want to partner me when we country danced, so maybe I could rely on them.

So, who won?

You know, don't you?

I came second. And to put it into context, even I voted for Alan.

I failed to understand that this meant that I too was a popular lad, after all I was second, not last or without a vote. I firmly believe that this event had a lasting effect on my morale, my confidence, my attitude to others.

By now you might be wondering what had happened to my fledgling career as a topflight footballer.

The teams were announced in the local press, the Citizen, and there for all to see was my name at full back, my accustomed position. Alan was selected as our centre forward. My job would be to tackle or intercept, and get the ball upfield to Al as quickly as possible. My health was holding up thankfully, and I anxiously awaited my date with fame.

I think the trial was set for the Wednesday, and it was around teatime on the Tuesday that I started sneezing. Oh shit! Not that I swore at eleven years of age, but you get my drift. I was far too polite to swear, too well brought up. And I was scared of what my father would do to me if he heard me, even under my breath. In all the years I knew him, I never once heard my dad swear in front of mum. And that went for me too.

But once I had sneezed, I recognised that there was no way back: there was no way my mother would allow me to run around a muddy football pitch with a cold, tantamount to the clarion call for pneumonia in her eyes. Mum was never particularly well herself, though this could easily be the subject of a four-part series of books. Best left.

And on the rocks of my bright red nose, my football future foundered. In big school, they would play rugby, and I didn't kick a soccer ball in anger for 7 years.

2. I ALMOST SKIPPED UNIVERSITY!

My primary school was in a particularly poor area of Churchdown, handily placed for me to get to easily, but some way from the village centre, where most local children attended the main Churchdown village school. I had been the brightest light in a dull uninspiring class. When we took the 11 plus, out of a class of 30, only 4 of us had passed, and most of us, as a result, had gone to the local secondary modern. Ironically, this was much closer to home than the grammar, which lay at the far end of the main village, and which was predominantly populated by kids from the village junior school and from neighbouring Brockworth and Hucclecote.

These were the 'big boys' – well, girls too, to be fair. It is perhaps unsurprising given the ease with which I had sailed through junior school, that grammar school came as a shock to my system. Indeed, come the end of the first year and my first school report, Mr Gaunt, the maths teacher and form tutor, suggested that in coming 14th in class he felt that Malcolm should have been capable of much more.

As I made the transition from junior to senior school, did I concentrate on making people laugh, to befriend others? My success at exams had not made me popular, so maybe I would be happier in my own skin by being one of the 'also rans'? Did I stop right then making the effort to be that child genius, to be 'top' once more? Did I compensate for my perceived lack of popularity by allowing my educational standards to slip? Or, was it simply that, whilst I had been a big fish in the smallest of ponds, once I made it to the great Atlantic Ocean that grammar school represented, I became way out of my depth?

But the fact that Wendy Fuller had beaten me, and everyone else for that matter, to top in class, didn't mean that I had not made an effort. My health had improved vastly and my absences totalled no more than a couple of weeks, and yet my 3rd in French was my finest effort. I was in the top set, but not 'top', and although this seemed to matter to the staff, I was happy enough to be average. For goodness sake, 14th out of over 120 in my year was good enough wasn't it? Especially when, to my mind, there were popularity contests to be won.

I remained in top class, moving seamlessly from class 1A to 2A, occasionally surprising both myself and my form tutor by excelling at one of the subjects, before returning to anonymity the following term. I would be good at French, then English Language, perhaps English Literature next, then German. Never geography. I just did not get on with the geography teacher and he certainly was no admirer of MH.

A pattern began to emerge of a student happy enough to be midstream in the premier set.

I had my moments of glory, oh yes.

The rugby teacher doubled up in Biology lessons, and also doubling up was the P E teacher, known to us all simply as 'The Red' because of the colour of his complexion, particularly when angry, and he was a stickler for rules. He frightened the living daylights out of most of the boys, despite being pretty short, perhaps five foot five in his stockinged feet.

We took P E twice a week, if you had remembered your kit and if your hair wasn't too long. The Red had a neat short back and sides, and, even in the era of the Beatles, expected everyone to do the same. I have known him to bring kids to tears just by holding them by the hair surrounding their ears and gently lifting them from the floor in an effort to convince them that it might be time for a trim.

In those days there was a lot of equipment; boxes, medicine balls, ropes to climb, bars to hang from, horses to jump, and mats. And so many exercises to perfect. Hanging from wall bars with feet out in front of your body so that your legs formed a right angle with your upper body. Torture. Count to ten, then hold it. Hold it. One more second, and breathe. Stomach muscles shaking, arms aching. If you had missed a lesson or two it felt even worse because you were out of practice. And you felt sick for days to come.

One of the favourite exercises back in the 60s was the crab. To do the crab you lay on your back, inverted your hands above your shoulders, and with your feet flat to the floor lifted your stomach towards the ceiling. The more half circular you appeared the better you were performing your crab. I was slim, bordering on thin, and I could do a crab. 'Look at Harris' the Red would shout. 'He's doing it right. Push, Harris. Yes, look at Harris'.

And all that time I would be extending hands and feet and pushing my torso up towards the ceiling, pride rushing through my very being that I had been picked out as an example of sheer brilliance. It gave me that momentary boost to my mediocre ego, that I was approaching perfection. It didn't last, and who knows what damage that particular exercise was doing to my spine. Needless to say, the crab is now frowned upon as potentially harmful.

I tried very hard to be popular, not to insight envy or hate. I saw myself as the Range Rider's companion Dick, Watson to his Holmes, Tonto to the Lone Ranger, a faithful sidekick in other words. I latched on to the popular kids, hanging around but saying little, in the hope that a little of their popularity would rub off on me. I ran errands, acted as a go-between on lover's trysts and spats, buttered people up, because at the time I genuinely believed that if you were nice to folk, they would like you in return. And pretty girls would find you attractive, because I firmly believed that the prettier the girl, the kinder and more honest she was. I was in for a big disappointment wasn't I!

The Swinging Sixties eh! Drugs and sex and rock and roll, nudge nudge, say no more. Bear in mind, that having been born in 1952, the Sixties came just that bit too soon for me. I was still growing up. Even when the Sixties came to a close, I was only 18, and a fairly naïve 18 at that.

I liked the Beatles. I got somewhat embarrassed when Paul wondered why we didn't 'do it in the road', even if 'no-one will be watching us'. Sex for me, was getting a kiss and wondering why girls got 'frustrated' when I didn't go far enough for their liking. As for drugs, I must have been 17 before I even tasted a half of bitter at a wedding reception, and I hated it. There were fads, like using the new word for liking someone – 'fancying a bird'. Cigarettes were passed around in the sixth form rest room. And some kids tried out glue.

I was too scared of the consequences. After all, children had died sniffing glue. The staff warned us about it. And I took heed.

I also refused to try out the deliberate fainting phase.

I don't recall exactly how it worked. What I do remember was that during break-time half a dozen of the braver (foolhardy?) kids amongst us were breathing out then crouching down frog-like, before springing up on to their feet. The lack of oxygen in their system brought about a sudden light-headedness and they passed out. It caught on rapidly, and we took it in turns to 'have a go'. Except that I was happy enough to stand around and gawp, and possibly help the fainters back to their feet, but perfectly content not to give it a try myself. Safety first.

I was shy and scared of my own shadow. I disliked being told off, especially if I thought I was innocent. If I did get caught out chatting in class, and that was just about the only naughty thing I did – no, sorry, there was one incident – it was always someone else's fault. They started it. Never me. I knew that if mum or more likely dad found out I had been bad I would be for it. Not physically, but dad could make me feel rotten just by knowing about things. And I did not want to let him down.

Dad had a strange influence over me. If we went to town, usually Gloucester, but sometimes Cheltenham, I would march alongside him, constantly looking up to his broad shoulders for approval. He would have a shopping list and make his way logically from one item to the next, plotting his route carefully from one shop to another which he often had written in brackets after the item, 'pay mortgage – (Council Offices)'.

I usually had nothing on my list, but just now and then I would need a new ruler or pen, or maybe a 45rpm single. Dad would never say, 'Don't buy that' but he would say things like, 'Do you really want that Beatles single?' or 'Why don't you save up for something else?' and it was rare that I actually bought the thing I had gone shopping for, such was his influence on me. I recall buying a Beach Boys extended play instead of a single I wanted, because it had 4 songs on it and offered better value, though it did have 'God only knows', 'Sloop John B' and 'Wouldn't it be Nice' on it, and ultimately became one of my most played records.

I always found authority a difficult issue once I left home, treating anyone I worked with as a father-figure, but never really knowing how far to rely upon them, or talk back at them, finding it altogether too tempting to react against their advice and take alternative action.

I rarely partied or went out, except to town. My spare time took me on to or around the green outside our house, either playing football or cricket, or running and cycling round the island. There, we had a clan of friends who took part in endless football matches that lasted well after sunset, or formed sprint teams to run relays against one another, just me from the grammar school, trying to fit in with the kids from the local secondary modern and doing it pretty well but sensing exclusion from the daily walk to school and shared conversations. I would arrive home from school on my bike to find that the secondary lads were already playing out. I had to have my tea and more than likely a ton of homework to do.

There was jealousy on both sides. They were jealous of my education, me of their freedom from homework overload. I was jealous of how close the secondary modern was to my house, they were jealous of our university places, jobs and salary potential. Gradually, more of the estate locals attended the grammar school, and I stopped being the odd one out.

The island came with ready-made goals at either end. Trees and the occasional telegraph pole formed goalposts with about 40 yards between them, ideal for us to set up football matches which lasted hours on end, players coming and going, scores into the teens or higher, well into the evening, with the floodlighting from lamp-posts coming on at sunset. I would ignore the calls to 'come in now' from mum, and only retire, sweat dripping from my vest, when dad got involved much later, light almost completely gone. Sometimes the grass would already be damp from overnight mist and our socks and shoes were sodden and had to be dried in front of the fire for tomorrow's match, newspaper stuffed into each shoe.

Or if we were playing 'tracking', our games could go on well after the last rays of sun had vanished below the horizon, which made spotting the chalk arrows really hard to trace. To play tracking one or two of us would run off, clutching a ball of chalk pinched from the remains of the post-war prefab walls knocked down to make way for new housing near the junior school. Every so often we would chalk an arrow on the ground or wall indicating the direction we were headed. It was up to the followers to 'track' us down and tag us by touching any part of the body when they located us. As the 'fastest runner' I would be sent back down the trail to peep around corners to see whether we were being followed, before turning tail and running back to join the hunted. Games often ended with a walk down to the nearest chippie for a takeaway and a bottle of pop before we raced home to make the 10 o'clock deadline.

In spite of considerable success at these harmless night-time games I was still relatively shy. My shyness was particularly apparent in my interaction with the fairer sex, to the extent that there truly wasn't much interaction at all. Whilst I was slim and fit, I was also spotty, and my fine hair had the tendency to turn greasy after a day without washing it. Not a dreamboat by any means.

I was not aware of how to treat girls and couldn't see a come-on if it stared me in the face. One girl who often sat behind me in lessons started up a conversation with me about a big rugby match taking place at the Gloucester Rugby Club featuring the touring Springboks at a time when apartheid and demonstrations against it were at their height. She asked if I was going. I said that I was going with my father and she suggested that perhaps if we were in town at the same time we could meet up. Totally oblivious to any charms young redhead Cathy had, I replied that I didn't think so, and that sadly was that. I believe that my first thought had been whether I could get away from my father's company with a legitimate excuse that didn't include a young girl or a date. I was far too embarrassed to simply tell the truth about the situation even at the tender age of eleven.

Just a reminder that you mentioned an incident at school?

Ah yes. You see, teachers failed to understand us kids back then. I had known Chris for ever. We went back to infant school and, as you will remember, she had accompanied me to 'big school'. We weren't always in the same class as our choices had sent us in different directions but, just now and again, our paths would cross, and we would be involved in silly banter. Banter often led to pushes, shoves and the occasional flick of the foot towards rear ends, all jokingly and in good spirit. But to Mr Protheroe, girls were girls, and boys should not mistreat them. I wholeheartedly agree with the sentiment, but Chris and I were pals, almost incidental to us what our individual sexes were. We were just messing about prior to class as we stood next to each other in line, arguing over nothing important.

Mr P failed to see the humour. As I say, he didn't understand that friends just did that, and he called out my name. I froze, but had to thaw sufficiently to make my way sheepishly into the biology lab for a dusting down. I wondered whether Chris would come to my rescue, calling out to the teacher that it was just a bit of childish fun. She didn't, and I was admonished, while obviously I had done nothing wrong. I never did, remember.

I spent too much time in my teens dreaming about a girl one year my junior. If I saw her at assembly it made my day, so you can imagine how excited I was whenever we spoke. She lived on the estate, one whole road away, and I used a special code to mark my diary if I was lucky enough to bump into her during the day.

I used to time my bike ride home to coincide with her long walk home if she decided to give the bus a miss, so that I could bump into her on the way and scoot alongside her 'til we got home, chatting about this and that, but patently getting nowhere, and merely upsetting myself when she mentioned James or Tony or David, whoever her latest boyfriend was. The advent of James led me to go out and buy Manfred Mann's latest single,

'Semi-detached suburban Mr James'. And all that time, other girls just got the cold shoulder, or, like Cathy, totally ignored.

That was, until Susan Jill Hanman came bobbying into view. At lunch, she occasionally acted as a meal monitor, carrying the tray of food and plates from the kitchen hatch to her table of 8, and passing my table with a spirited wiggle and a fetching smile. And a mini-skirt. Her smile was almost as infectious as her legs were long and, to my innocent eyes, so very sexy, and I was smitten.

But in a weird twist of events, I did not go out with my Sue until I had met, dated and unceremoniously dumped Lorna.

I was lost property prefect, a position of the highest trustworthiness. This meant hanging about the lost property cupboard at lunchtimes when nobody else was allowed in the building unless it was raining. It was here that I met Lorna. She was petite and really quite cute. We chatted innocently, enjoying each other's company. She told me she originated from the Isle of Man. I was from Wales, and somehow our origins outside the county brought us closer together. So, in a brave move, I asked her to come to a school production with me.

I was totally unclear how this would work in practice. I couldn't tell my parents. I just couldn't. So, ostensibly going out alone, I arranged to meet Lorna around the corner, on her route to school from her house across the main road. Without transport, and not trusting local buses, we walked the

41

3 miles to school, dawdling along on a warm evening and chatting all the way.

Three and a half hours later I walked her home as far as the main road but no further. I have forgotten most of the detail, but she did mention her father, the police and being watched, so best not cross the road with her. I had already begun to feel uncomfortable about one or two things she had said regarding her father and his drinking habits, so it came as no surprise when I left her at my side of the main road, and made my way home.

That would have been that, except that unbeknown to me, Sue had also had a date that evening with my classmate John. They had attended the same school production, was it the Mikado? As we had left the main hall I bumped into Sue, who offered me a lift home in her dad's Rover. I gratefully declined, but from that night on we were best of buddies. I could sense, for once, flirtation in that proposal of hers.

I cycled to Sue's house and back countless times that summer, up and down country lanes, trying to stay cool but arriving at her place with my shirt stuck firmly to my back, my fashionable fringe plastered to my forehead. I must have looked a real catch. I was lucky in that it rarely rained that summer.

I had previously held hands with Lorna of course, but my first kiss was with Sue, a quick but gentle brushing of lips on a short walk along the main road in her village. Most of the time we were chaperoned by her younger sister Helen, but just that once we somehow got away on our own. That kiss, a milestone in my courting history, was immediately followed by a joint decision to go back to her place before drizzle got any heavier. One kiss was clearly enough to signal our intentions to 'go out with one another'. In modern terminology we were no longer single.

We did manage to get away to the fair in Gloucester on one glorious afternoon in August but even then, we had a certain young lady in tow. Her mum thought that young men were only after one thing and unashamedly employed young Helen to keep an eye on us. She was undoubtedly right in respect of most young men, but far from the mark as far as I was concerned. I thought I was finally in love, and an equal dose of naivety and respect prevented me from going too far.

I worked nights that summer, in the largest ice-cream factory in Europe, packaging lollies and mousses. I was slow and cumbersome, but the pay was good, and work colleagues fun and friendly. It meant, though, that Sue and I could spend most days together, whenever it was convenient to her parents that is. My mum and dad took to Sue straight away, and invited her on days out in our new Morris 1000 car during the school holidays. We talked about the future.

University loomed large for me. I admit now to not trying my hardest in my 'A' levels, because although I would have been the first in my estate to have gone to university, I was loathed to leave Sue. She was my first real love, and part of me wanted just to quit school and get employment. I had been expected to go to university by teachers at a school that was still in its infancy. A few of the previous year's intake had been fortunate to go off to uni, but our year offered the prospect of a good number of college students and I was one of them. Don't get me wrong, I studied hard, buying myself revision cards, 'Key Facts', and reading them over and over again, but I would often daydream and find myself dropping off to sleep as I revised in my bedroom, before waking up an hour or two later, cold and bemused. I was quite prepared not to pass.

I needn't have worried, because I still qualified for uni. In fact, Swansea University rang to say they would accept me, despite my failure to achieve their minimum requirement. It was just in time to pip 'Cardiff', whose more generous terms I had met and whose campus I was preparing to make home when Swansea's offer came through.

Sue and I exchanged letters on a regular basis. Envelopes bore the iconic 'ITALY' mnemonic in the top corner, and letters were SWALK, sometimes splashed with the day's favourite perfume. We missed one another and couldn't wait for Christmas. I remained loyal, but by the time I came home for the holidays, Sue had more or less come to the sad conclusion that our relationship, such as it was, was doomed to failure and, after some discussion over whether we could salvage it, we split up. I sobbed for days.

I had no idea what she meant when she said she was 'frustrated' and had to move on. We weren't getting anywhere, and with me away and only coming home every so often there really was no future for us. Sue rightly expected more from any relationship she had. She needed constant reassurances about her femininity, and for that she had to have her boyfriend close at hand. More than anything she wanted to be loved.

What I failed to grasp was that Sue was a mature 16 and a half and I was 18 going on 14. After all, this was the same lad who, in the school civics lesson, sat in wonder as teacher and sixth-form pupils discussed how much a packet of 3 was now. 3 WHAT for goodness sake? Naïve did I say?

Before Sue came along, kids at school had talked incessantly about their boy and girl friends. New words for me were 'fancy' and 'go'. Did I fancy so and so, did I think that she goes. I wasn't entirely sure what we were talking about. There were girls I quite liked, the pretty ones, who were bound to be the nice respectable ones, but what was this fancying? Did they go? Where exactly? As I say, I spent a lot of time acting as a runner for my friends, dashing between boys and girls taking messages, just like the 'go-between'. I tried to befriend the girls by being on their side whilst trying not to lose the boys' goodwill. Tricky ground and like walking on eggshells. I walked the tightrope of friendship and, in the event, suffered from a loss of real pals. In retrospect, I reckon that I must have badmouthed the boys to their wannabee girlfriends so that I looked good and would maybe appeal to them instead, without the guts to ask them out myself.

I am pretty sure I would not have known where to invite them for a date. Very few of my classmates lived in my village, or at least my end of the village. Dad had no transport other than his pushbike at that time, though he did hire a car for our summer holidays sometimes. I could have met them in town I suppose, but what could I have offered them when I received limited pocket money.

We weren't poor but dad had been obliged to work nights when we arrived in Churchdown to make ends meet, having bought his own house on a council mortgage. I believe that uncle Roy had been kind enough to subsidise some of my Christmas presents in order to make the Season jolly, so I was not ideally placed to show a girl a good time, and had no confidence in my own charms to simply be with someone for a chat over coffee.

I no longer had the feeling of being the 'boy wonder'. I had lost the one quality that made me different, that enabled me to stand out from the crowd, that made me interesting. One thing had become certain: I was not the child genius some had imagined me to be. I had found my place in mid-table. My 'averageness' was now obvious for all to see, except that now my audience was even larger.

My perception was undeniably flawed. It was my perception that I was placed midway in my class, and this in itself was perfectly correct, but what I had failed to take into account was that I was already attending the grammar school, representing perhaps the top 30% of my age-group. In addition, there were 4 classes in my year, and of those I was in the top class, putting me firmly in the top 10%. By finishing halfway down the ranks of the top group I was well within the first 5%, and genuinely better than 'average'. University would perhaps enable me to put things in perspective.

3. I ALMOST MISSED A COMPLETE YEAR!

It was the summer of 1972. I was halfway through a four-year degree course at Swansea University, one of the colleges that made up the University of Wales. 'Abertawe' to give it its rightful Welsh name, 'at the mouth of the River Tawe'.

Right on the coastline, and minutes from the lovely Gower Coast, Swansea University could not have been better placed to study, with just a dual carriageway separating the campus from the golden sandy beach to the south, and with Singleton Park bordering the campus to the north. Idyllic.

But it was not to be the location for year 3 of my degree course. I had studied a combination of English, French and German in my first year while I made the final decision on my degree subject. I applied to take an honours degree in French, but to my surprise my results in German had exceeded my expectations, and I was wavering between the two. The prospect of spending my third year abroad in either France or Germany steered me towards French, and so it was that I applied to spend the third year anywhere in the Loire Valley. Somewhere near Tours if at all possible.

There I would have the comfort of being near big towns such as Tours itself, Angers and Blois, be near to nature, in the midst of chateau country, and in the heart of French culture, not to mention Côtes de Rhône wines, to which I had become very accustomed, and, some would say, (un)reasonably attached. I had no car at the time, in fact I couldn't yet drive, and so being close to all other modes of transport seemed vital if I was going to be able to take full advantage of my time away.

Just about everyone in the French class would be invited to work abroad for three terms, either in Universities or in secondary schools as *'assistants'* and employed by local authorities on a salary. To a student on a grant the prospect was thrilling, and I looked forward to discovering the whereabouts of my posting. News of my placement would arrive by letter.

I thought that in my application I had made some salient points about just where I wanted to be, my lack of transport, the need to be near a big town with good links, my love of history and culture, (not mentioning the wine!) and so I was confident that I would be granted my wish. My pal Tim had already received his letter of appointment. He was heading to Carcassonne in the south west of France where the influence of Spanish was readily noticeable in speech and customs, a lovely big walled town with an influx of tourists including English, so I knew he would be happy with this.

Flap went the letter box, and I knew instinctively what it would be. Records were broken as I flew down the stairs to the front door. Rip went the envelope. And there it was. The town I was heading for was...........La

Ferté-Macé with two acute accents over the final two 'e's. Where in the name of goodness was THAT! I couldn't recall seeing La Ferté on my Loire Valley map, so, out came the atlas, and my index finger began to trawl across the map of France in an ever-increasing circle around Tours. Minutes passed. And then, buried deep in the department of Orne, I found it. In Normandy. North of Tours, north of Le Mans, heading for the Normandy World War 2 beaches, but before hitting the only civilised town I had come across in Normandy, Caen.

It looked like a small town, so I felt sure it would have amenities, shops, sports facilities and transport links. Back in the day, before the advent of anything vaguely technologically useful, you had to rely on books, brochures or leaflets to inform you about foreign shores, and I wrote to the French Tourist Board for as much as they could tell about my new home town.

Along with some pretty brochures about Normandy, I received a train timetable which I knew would come in extremely useful. And before you predict that La Ferté had no railway station, let me assure you, that was the first thing I checked.

Before we were allowed to descend upon the unassuming French public, or more to the point, the French education system, we were invited to attend the most elite of French Universities in Paris, the Sorbonne. Now, I had actually heard of the Sorbonne, and was duly impressed with its giant classrooms and lecture halls. We were staying in student digs in the suburbs of Paris in Nanterre.

I don't think I will ever forget, or for that matter, recover from, the walk from the railway station to the student quarters, two tall university residential blocks way over there in the distance.

When I left home in England, I had the foresight to send a trunk containing clothes, books (especially my large English-French dictionaries) and tape machine on ahead by rail. In theory, therefore, I merely had a couple of lighter cases with which to pass the week in Paris and get me started in school for the first week or so.

Growing up, I had often heard my parents muttering the words "Just in case", usually in respect of items popped into the attic, or, more usually, the garage. This would happen moments after it looked for all the world as if they were being consigned to the dustbin. Now, all of a sudden, I understood the deep meaning of these three, individually insignificant, words, when used in this phrase, in this order. And in view of the containers in which I was about to transport almost all my worldly belongings, a more appropriate phrase could not have been imaginable.

Sweaters, polo necks, scarves, gloves, more socks, shirts and underpants were added to the pile, you know, just in case. In case of what I cannot begin to tell you. Famine, another ice age, a worldwide shortage of underpants, who knows?

But I do know, that when I stepped from the train at Nanterre with what seemed like five miles to walk, those two cases (plus a rucksack, containing more just-in-cases) weighed a ton. And to ensure that my bags did not split open on the journey we had surrounded each case with a leather strap which scraped against the outside of each knee as I bundled along in 10-yard bursts before depositing one case at a time on the hot pavement.

Needless to say, the sun was shining, and sweat dripped from my forehead, plastering my still fashionable fringe to my skin, just as it had done on my cycle journeys to Sue's house. The handles were moulded plastic, the cases now twice as heavy as I had anticipated when I tested them out back in blighty, and my fingers struggled to close around the grips, gradually lengthening until they turned a whiter shade of pale and dropped the bag again and again. I fell behind the rest of my group. Just to add insult to injury, the knobbly end of one of the handles popped out of its feeble metal housing. I had stressed it to its limit, and my walk became all the harder, now dragging one case along on its thick cardboard edges. No cases with wheels in those days. You can't imagine how grateful I was to reach the shade of the two tower blocks and to rest my aching fingers.

Thankfully, not all my experiences in Normandy were quite so difficult or painful.

The headmistress was also the English teacher, and she spoke English almost as well as I. In a way, this was detrimental, for I found myself tempted to speak to her in my native tongue rather than risk making an idiot of myself by attempting to converse in my schoolboy French.

Of course, the kids took the piss out of my accent, especially my version of the "u" sound which to them sounded like the impression of an owl. And they sniggered gently whenever I said 'tu' (you). By the same token, I managed not to smile when they said 'ello' and dropped the aitch from my surname.

The lycée at La Ferté-Macé was a senior school for pupils from 16 years of age upwards, so I use the word 'kids' loosely. Some of my kids were as old as me and I was 20! The explanation was that the school was made up of two separate and diverse streams. The first stream was what I expected, concentrating on a general wide-ranging syllabus. The second, but no less important, focussed on technical subjects, and pupils wore smocks and aprons over their one-piece overalls, often messy from contact with wood, ironwork and coals.

To achieve their baccalaureate, some less accomplished students were kept back one or two years to repeat their course, particularly in English. I found it odd that someone should have to learn a foreign language before they could make progress with their career in technology.

However, I must say that they were the most enthusiastic pupils of the lot. They were always happy to have a go and use the little English they had. I spent many happy hours chatting with these – mainly lads – during their breaks. Footballers of the day formed the basis of most of our discussions, such as Bobby Charlton and Bobby Moore, this being not a million years since England's last big success of 1966. Who was my favourite player, which was my favourite team? They introduced me to syrupy drinks of all colours and hues, laughed at my jokes, and listened intently as I told them about my life in England. They seemed fascinated by my choice of music, and seemingly all knew a line or two of Beatles music, especially 'Hey Jude' for some reason.

On one particular occasion, I was drifting back to my digs, and was due to meet up with one of the teachers in a few minutes time, when a group of my 'fans' decided it was time that I joined them in their lesson, as their teacher had failed to turn up. We stood outside the classroom portacabin having a spirited debate about my availability.

"But I have to be somewhere" I ventured.

Yes, with them, they said imploringly.

No, seriously, I had a meeting.

Who with? As if it made any difference.

Smiling as they did, they closed in on me, forming a circle around me like Indians round the cowboy wagons I had seen on television westerns.

I was not in any danger, I knew that, but I DID have a meeting to go to, so smiling back I tried to reason with them.

Come on, be fair, "Je ne peux pas……" I offered meekly, "I can't".

"Mais oui" came the reply, and without so much as a how's your father
– try explaining that one to a French lad – they grabbed me and swept me
off my feet, before lifting me unceremoniously above their heads, and
carting me off to the door of their classroom.

I only escaped once they realised that, without their teacher, they could
not access the room and that we would have to remain outside 'en plein air'.
To be honest, I was thankful that they did not twig that I had a set of door
keys in my pocket, and off to my meeting I went with just the faintest of self-
satisfied grins. Somebody appreciated me!

Talking of which, I was at that age when relationships with the opposite
gender tend to be at their peak, and at the Sorbonne one of the lasting
instructions I received was, not, under any circumstances, to get 'involved'
with any of the pupils. Now I would guess that 70% of my pupils were lads,
so the odds had already been diminished for me, but coupled with that, I
always did as I was told, so the chance that I would disobey my commands
was pretty slim. However, the 30% on offer did present me with the odd
dilemma, with one such predicament as rapidly as just 5 days into my stay.

One of the girls in my grammar class approached me with a note after
class, inviting me to an evening in a nearby town, Alençon, where she
informed me other *assistants d'anglais* would be meeting up. Her mother
and father would be driving and I could travel in the back of the car with
her. I felt certain that it would have been an enjoyable evening, comparing
notes with other British students abroad, but the prospect of starting my

year in the back seat of a car with a lively 16-year-old girl raised the dreadful prospect of criticism and reprimand.

I politely declined.

I have to admit now, that had the girl in question been Marie-Laure, a cheeky young blonde in the same year, my answer might well have been different. Marie-Laure was what is probably best described as a tease, always speaking out of turn, poking fun at me and gesturing delightfully when I got things wrong. I have a group photo in which she can be seen slightly to my rear waving two fingers behind my head in the trademark imitation of bunny ears.

Don't get me wrong, I did have my escapades, but with a lovely American girl I met at the Sorbonne, and a very attractive French lass whose father worked on a tug boat out of Le Havre. Both of these long-distance affairs dwindled away when the girls both decided to pursue relationships closer to home, rather than commit to a prospect of moving abroad. Naturally I never envisaged living 'chez elles' in their country.

I didn't return home at Christmas, in spite of mum's desire to see her lad again, but the prospect of spending the holiday with two young women, North American students just my senior in years, on a train journey to Rome via Paris, marginally won out. We visited the Vatican and the Roman Coliseum, ate in local pizzeria and attended St Peter's on Christmas Day, entering the basilica on a dull morning and emerging to a miraculously bright and sunny day. I thought attending a papal audience would be a thrill of a lifetime, and would make the sacrifice of not going home worthwhile in itself. Home would still be there waiting for me, and besides, I was young and enjoying my foreign adventure. I will never forget seeing St Peter's in glorious sunshine, or the Colosseum rising majestically through the early morning mist.

The holidays were not the only time I could get away though.

Fortunately enough for me, the *assistant* in nearby Alencon, Nick Rose, had his own car, and we regularly met up in the spring of 1973 to enjoy jaunts in the French countryside, travelling to Tours, La Baule, Les Sables d'Olonne and Saint-Malo.

We camped everywhere we went, pitched our tents in pouring rain, drank milk 'straight from the cow' in farmers' fields, visited chateaux, and generally mixed with the locals. Genuinely the most enjoyable time.

Michel, who was an English teacher at the next-door junior school, took me to witness the charms of Mont-St-Michel, parking on the notoriously deadly sands, and rushing back to the car before the tide did the same.

xxxxxxxxxxxxxxxxxxxxxxxxxxx

The school year, which had seemed interminable as it lay ahead of me in October, sped by, and it was soon time to leave my new friends.

And when it finally arrived, my last day at the school was touching. The headmistress called me into class with the grammar stream to present me with a wrapped and ribboned box of goodies, including humorous books, biscuits, chocolates and a bottle of local wine, plus a litre of the finest Normandy calvados.

This was the same classroom where some months before I had stammered and blushed in front of the same teacher and pupils.

To lighten the intensity of her English lessons, Madame P had decided to bring in some music. The intention was that we would play some modern songs and try to translate the words. A great idea, in principle. There are just so many great songs in the English language.

By the way, I admit that even though I was fairly fluent, many songs I heard in France were pretty meaningless, words in local dialect, phrases sung too quickly, loud music. I had my favourites though. I particularly liked, and in fact bought, 'Himalaya' by C.Jérome, complete with cheery bagpipes, despite my intense dislike of that instrument.

I also bought a duetted single disc of Brigitte Bardot and Sacha Distel singing a French language version of Stevie Wonder's 'You are the sunshine of my life', probably just for the cover photo (no, of Brigitte Bardot, thank you).

By extension, I did struggle with 2 and a bit-hours of dubbed-flick, 'The French Connection' complete with Marseille dialect, but it didn't stop me from visiting the local cinema once in a while. It was a way of passing time, though I didn't always fully understand what was going on in the films.

And these films, and others, were advertised in the café opposite the school on colourful posters. To decorate my apartment walls, I fancied one or two of these bright posters, like the Clint Eastwood westerns, James Bond movies, and musicals, and was therefore obliged to drink a few 'pernods' while I chatted to the proprietor, on the scrounge.

He was as good as gold. He replaced his adverts weekly, and stored the old ones all rolled up together and elastic- banded for me to collect, so that I didn't even need to stop for a drink. Though, don't you think that it would have been rude to ignore his kind offer to hang around his café and drink fine alcohol? Exactly my reasoning too.

Back in the classroom, Madame P had her own favourites too, it seemed. I had always been a tune man. Never too bothered by what the lyrics were, after all you could hum along to almost any song. Elvis was all hubba hubba, Jagger na-na-nasal, Bowie wo-wo-weyey, McCartney Ooh Ooh Yeah, so I could imitate them all in my own way. Some singers I couldn't fathom. Americans especially. Dylan was one.

"Today we are going to try and translate a great English song" she began. "It's by one of the best performers in the world."

I hesitated.

I had the strangest of feelings.

It was going to be Dylan.

And the song, 'Lay lady lay'.

Oh, good, I said, while internally screaming "Nooooooooo!"

As well as finding Dylan could be notoriously vague with his pronunciation – was it a grass bed or a brass bed? – I realised how embarrassing the lyrics were going to prove to a mixed class of 16-year-olds as we dissected them line by line, 'until the break of day', bless him.

On we ploughed, discussing in some detail who this related to and what they were doing on the grass / brass bed until dawn broke.

10 minutes gone and just 50 to go, I comforted myself.

'Let me see ya make him smile', we went on. His hands are clean, oh gosh, why do we need to know that?

On and on, word by word, still laying, the one she loved now standing in front of her.

No, please kids, don't ask why he was standing.

Not long to go now surely?

Just long enough apparently to include "I long to reach for you in the night" and for me to take my leave, with sweat dribbling down the back of my trendy, and incredibly aptly named, polo neck sweater.

And they say teaching is an art.

I suppose you will want to know whether I was any good at this teaching lark. After all this book is about my perceived failure to excel, so you might expect me to be a really average 'teach'.

When the first term commenced, I took the lessons seriously. I was keenly aware of my responsibility. To support the teaching staff with the solemn process of getting the kids through their exams. I was given some rough rules to follow. But no guidance regarding the lessons.

My first lessons demonstrated the wide range in ability I was faced with. The grammar classes were interested, keen to exchange thoughts and views in English where possible. Teacher remained in the room and supervised, which made for a somewhat uncomfortable atmosphere at times. I prepared structured lessons, making full use of the blackboards to draw crosswords, write clues and explain grammatical issues. I made the hour as much fun as I could, raising a laugh with my attempts at a local Normandy dialect and with my regional British accents such as Cockney and Welsh.

That didn't last!

Teacher found that she could trust me with the pupils on my own, and so took a backseat, to such an extent that I now took the lessons by myself, without supervision. From now on I adopted a more leisurely approach, sitting on a table at the front of the classroom and chatting about sport, television, customs and so on.

I can hear you asking yourself whether I ever considered taking up the teaching profession. Don't get me wrong, I really enjoyed the experience. I loved the kids. Teaching appealed to me. I even once stood in as college lecturer for a friend who fell ill. It lasted only a few weeks but it confirmed for me how difficult the profession could be. The preparation for each lesson took so much time and effort, deciding how to present the information, how to get the students on board, how to set homework and mark it, and to get it back to the students on time again. So, I guess the truthful answer is 'No'. Teaching wasn't for me.

You are maybe now wondering about the title of this chapter? And how on earth I could easily have missed the foreign experience altogether?

You may remember that my group from uni were billeted in Nanterre for a week's preparatory grounding at the Sorbonne? Don't forget that I had with me the SNCF (French Railways) official time-tables, with trains for the summer up to 30 September 1972, coincidentally the date of my travel, and then, on the subsequent pages, from 1st October for the winter. This bulky document became dog eared and grubby from thumbing, as I constantly checked and rechecked the timings of my train from Paris to La Ferté.

I was just so pleased to discover that the town was served by the mainline to the capital. It would mean I would not be cut off during the long winter months, when I guessed that homesickness might kick in. Without my own transport, a train link was going to prove invaluable.

I took my cases into the Sorbonne with me on the suburban train on the last day of the course, so, saying goodbye and good luck to my fellow Swansea students, I set off for my train into the Normandy countryside.

La Ferté – Macé was the terminus for the train. I was tired after a hectic 7 days in Paris and I could therefore completely dismiss the fear of sleeping through and thus missing my stop. I dozed for what literally seemed a moment, before the train lurched to an abrupt halt.

Outside it was dark. Where were we? I couldn't see any signs, but I was certain the train was going no further. I gathered my bags up and opened the train door. No platform. Odd, but perhaps, seeing as we were out in the sticks, it made perfect sense?

It was a serious distance down on to the gravelled floor. I almost stumbled as I stepped from the train and feebly grabbed my cases. I wasn't quite with it. And now, to find out if anyone had come to meet me. If they had, I could not see them. No lights either?

Gradually I saw the light. I mean literally. Coming from the other side of the train windows. I started to redden, because I realised that the absence of a platform my side of the tracks meant one thing; I had got off on the wrong side of the train, and it was not about to pull out again.

I would have to walk to the back of the train and sheepishly poke my head around the guard's van to make my entry. Still, providing there was no welcoming committee I would escape embarrassment.

As deep as the step down had been, the step back up on to the platform was even steeper. And just as I staggered my weary way up to Platform One, two faces peered from the waiting room. A suited young man bearing a card label with the name Michel written on it in black felt-tip, and a station master, emerged smiling, with open arms ready to shake my hand.

Switch to French.

They welcomed me to France and tried to make light of my late arrival. I kind of understood. The station master looked at me and in a serious voice told me how lucky I was to have arrived at all. I smiled. After all he said this was the last train. Well, armed with my SNCF time-table, I already knew this. There had been no later train that day.

But no, he added, I was very lucky.

This was the last train.

Until Easter next year.

In my time-table, remember, I had checked the trains in the summer schedule. That ran to 30 September 1972 of course, the day of my journey. I hadn't needed to check trains from 1 October.

And it was just as well, because the schedule for the winter was blank, empty, non-existent. In short, La Ferté-Macé was a summer-only destination for Parisians, travelling mostly to Bagnoles, a pretty spa village 5 kilometres away. Bagnoles had its own casino, race track, lake and pump-rooms for the 'cure'. Once the summer was over, and Parisians were back at work, Bagnoles resumed its peaceful existence. If Parisians had no requirement for a train, well, it just got hooked.

I truly was fortunate, because had I delayed my journey by just one day, I would have COMPLETELY missed out on my French school adventure. Ah well, such is the life of a mere mortal!

Me and Chief Petty Officer Jack Harris. Below, cousin Trevor Hockey, front left.

First day at big school, too young for long trousers

How dad would have preferred to see me, with Carne, undefeated 1967.

Wednesday, March 20, 1963

GLOS'TER SCHOOLS PICK 49 FOR SOCCER TRIAL

THE following players have been chosen to participate in the trials held to decide the teams for the Gloucester Primary Schools' three inter-town soccer matches. Both games will take place at 10 a m on Saturday, February 23, at Coney Hill Junior School.

GAME 1

Red: G. Simpson (Whaddon); M. Harris (Parton-rd), T. Banks (Widden); R. Macdonald (Coney Hill), A. Buck (Brockworth), P. Hamilton (Whaddon); K. Ballinger (St. Paul's), A. Letts (St. James), A. Taylor (Parton-rd.), T. Hopkins (Finlay), D. Whitson (St James).

Blue: K. Taylor (Widden); T. Williams (Hucclecote), B. Stokes (Coney Hill); T. Edwards (Longlevens), C. Ashby (Widden), J. Taylor (St. James); R. Hickman (Widden), I. Collinson (St. Peter's), K. Ireland (Whaddon), R. Hart (Coney Hill), A. Henderson (Longlevens).

Referee: Mr. T. Smith (Finlay). Observers: Messrs. V. Willis, H. Selby. Replacements after 15 minutes: Goal, G. Arthur (Brockworth), left-half, R. Schultka (Hucclecote).

GAME 2

Purple and Gold: M. Long (Longlevens); J. Barnett (Coney Hill), R. Holder (The Moat); J. Browning (Elmbridge), P. Barter (Lower Tuffley), S. Rutland (Longlevens); J. Targett (Robinswood), M. Jones (Lower Tuffley), A. Cockburn (S. Peters), R. Walton (Elmbridge), J. Walsh (Robinswood).

Blue and White: D. Perkin (Robinswood); N. Evans (Elmbridge), N. Bozeat (Lower Tuffley); M. Walker (Robinswood), C. Gapp (Finlay), B. Hook (Elmbridge); D. Tiley (The Moat), M. Redding (Elmbridge), L. Lane (Lower Tuffley), G. Eden (Elmbridge), M. Hayes (Coney Hill).

Referee: Mr. G. Harris (Coney Hill) Observers: Messrs. A. Dallow, D. Bewley. Replacements after 15 minutes: Goal—L Hancock (Finlay) and D. Lyske (St. Peter's); left-half—J. Young (St. Peter's).

CITY PRIMARY SCHOOLS' FINE SOCCER

On Tuesday night the Gloucester Primary Schools' Association Football XI defeated Dursley by 3 goals to 1 on the Coney Hill Junior School ground.

Despite heavy rain both teams played attractive football and Gloucester soon took the lead when Walsh headed a brilliant goal.

This was shortly followed by a goal from Taylor, to give Gloucester a 2-0 lead at half-time.

In the second half Gloucester went further ahead through a fine opportunists goal by Taylor, and Dursley replied with a goal by Wilde.

The same team has been chosen to represent Gloucester versus Cheltenham today, at 5 p m, at Coney Hill Junior School, namely: M. Long (Longlevens); C. Gapp (Finlay), J. Barnett (Coney Hill); J. Browning (Elmbridge), T. Edwards (Longlevens), R. Macdonald (Coney Hill); R. Tangett (Robinswood), I. Collinson (St. Peter's), A. Taylor (Parton-rd.), A. Henderson (Longlevens), J. Walsh (Robinswood). Reserves: M. Walker (Robinswood), M. Hayes (Coney Hill). Referee: Mr. F. Morris.

Yes, that's me. Just a blur on the touchline.

And still running at Midland Bank Regional Sports Day thirty years later

Watch out David Bailey. My first ever photo taken at Weston-Super-Mare with dad's camera.

My chance to shine, ruined by a cold, and a too attentive mother.

My 'home' in Normandy, below, the pupils at the end of term, the café, the station, and the main street

Chosen Hill School. Above, a shot for publication in the local paper featuring the 'new' school. I am on the left, third face in, with my satchel.

Left, a prized photo of me with the Colts Second 15

Below, 1970 sixth form. The following year 'we' became a comprehensive school.

4. THE TOP SPORTSMAN I ALMOST BECAME

It would never have been half as important if Rob Jenkins had managed to complete his triple jump without injury. Rob and I were the Carne house team representatives in the triple jump, on the fateful school day in 1968. It was school sports day, and Rob was one of our team's best all-round and fastest competitors. I was quick down the runway, but my three elements were individually shorter, and, therefore, some 3 yards down on Rob's excellent leap. This left me in 8th place of 8, and pointless. If I was to be of any use to my house, I would need to improve drastically. But while Rob was performing so well, my score, such as it was likely to be, wouldn't count for much on the overall match total. Nonetheless, I prepared for my next leap. A few stretches, touch the toes, run on the spot.

It was then that I saw a gathering at the far end of the landing pit. It wasn't unusual for some competitors to tumble out of the end of the sand pit, and I guessed that Rob, or someone similarly gifted, had done exactly that. Whoever it was had regained their composure and was stood amidst the crowd, now moving away without any apparent limp, so if it was Rob at least he was uninjured. One or two younger pupils were racing amongst the teachers, no doubt spreading rumours of injury and near death.

In due course I would find out what was happening, and I had my turn on the runway in a few moments, so best concentrate on improving on my first effort.

I knew I had a quick run-up, but it was always a question of how near the board I could manage to place my take-off without red flagging. We didn't bother with all that marking the run-up lark like the pros did in the Olympics, just flung our track-suit tops down roughly where we wanted to start and set off like the clappers. Right, here we go.

Hang on though. Some of the teachers were looking concerned, more concerned than normal if you know what I mean. And there was now a palpable whisper that things were not quite as they should be. The rumour was that our best hope for the sprints and the relays had been injured, and that points would be hard to come by for Carne if the rumour was true. It appeared that in competing for Carne in the triple-jump, Rob Jenkins had somehow managed to spear his own hand with the spikes from one of his shoes. You can tell how seriously Rob took his athletics – spikes! And the rest of us wore daps or Green Flashes at best. Young Rob was said to be waiting for the ambulance, his participation in sports day at an abrupt and premature end.

Now we needed every point we could muster.

Charged with inspiration and sudden responsibility for the welfare of my house I set off down the gravel runway, building up speed and crossing my fingers that I would meet the take-off board just right. I hit the board. My hop was perfect, my step extended and high, the landing solid enough to enable me to launch into my jump. To be fair, my first two elements were always fairly reliable. I was pretty useless at the long-jump, so it was the final element of the triple-jump that had often let me down.

However, whether it was knowing the predicament Carne found itself in, or simply that the gods were with me that day, my jump took me way into the pit. Please don't fall back on landing now, Malc………..Get the tape measure on that one guys! It looked a reasonable distance to me, not a 'Rob' distance, but pretty damned fine for me.

The distances were not always announced straight away. They had to be passed by hand to a runner who would trot off to the announcer in the tiny p.a. tent. It gave the appearance of turning a thoroughly amateur afternoon into a semi-professional occasion. And the teacher with the best voiceover voice, usually the English teacher, would add gravitas to the whole event.

I cannot remember the exact distance now. After all, more than 50 years have passed since that grey afternoon – the sun rarely shone on sports day. It was far enough to promote me to third and into the points. And it remained my best effort in the sporting field, a third, but when the chips were down and team-mates were relying on me…… I was justly proud of my efforts, and continued to perform satisfying distances for many years, well into my university days, when I would often run along the beach at Swansea Bay and throw in the occasional triple.

Occasionally still, I dream of the triple jump. I will be on a beach or in a field, practising, scraping a take-off board in the ground and pacing out an imaginary run-up. Then I take off, and linger in the air with my hop, flying effortlessly above the sand or grass, foot after foot, yard after yard, a graceful step, again, yards of flight, and a final easy jump, my foot delaying its landing as it glides inches above the 'pit'. And down. And in my head, I convince myself that this is not a dream, that I have once again beaten my own record, only to awaken and realise that I have been dreaming. Poo!

Quick enough over the ground to have been a sprinter and a winger, but when it came to cross-country, that required stamina I just was not possessed of. Our cross-country course was long, and, to begin with, very hilly. In fact, it took us out of the school grounds, along local roads and into the fields at the base of Chosen Hill. From there a steep incline led up the hill until we reached the Norman church our school badge had emblazoned on it. We circled the church before plummeting down the other side of the hill at breakneck speeds, exceptionally slippery following heavy rain or frost. At the bottom, our course met a dual-carriageway under construction, and from there we traced a path along main roads until they took us back into the village and 'home'.

On occasions, I had spotted some of the elite runners deviating from the set course as they hit the new road by turning left across the fields. I was intrigued, as you would be, by their action, but most weeks trudged on, usually alone by now.

One week I must have thought to myself, "Well, if they are taking a short-cut, why don't I?" and although I was a few yards adrift of the backmarker, off I went! A decision I lived to regret.

By the time I saw the last man disappear through a hedge, I was lost, though I did try desperately to catch up with the shouts I heard coming from the group. My short-cut had let me down, and, what was worse, I was on my own. I wandered lonely as the proverbial cloud for minutes on end, searching for the route my school mates had taken, but to no avail. Rather than retreat to the road now, I imagined that there was bound to be a route back over the hill and so I squelched my way back up through muddy fields to the top of the hill, gasping for breath and wheezing ever so gently.

By now, both the cheats and most other runners had made their way back to school and were in the showers, hot first to dispel the mud, then cold, we never knew why.

Meanwhile I was paying my respects to the church once again. Then, back down the hillside, caked in mud, and on to the village roads. I felt as though I had completed two runs, and in fairness, I probably had.

I gasped my way into the changing rooms as if I had been smoking Gitanes all the way.

The Red stood before me.

Where had I been!

"Sorry, Sir, I somehow got lost."

Too late to shower, I just changed out of my filthy kit and into my uniform, and made my way home on my bike. I collapsed on to my bed and ran a welcome bath. When faced with the same choice on the next run I let the big boys enjoy their short-cut while I stuck to the road, and it was far quicker too.

I have already touched on my abortive football career. It is one of my biggest regrets that I didn't follow my dreams and play more football through my formative years. I did play the occasional game for my hall of residence at Uni, but football had moved on. No longer would I be able to play full-back or right half. You now played in a back four or in midfield. Even cousin Trevor Hockey had switched from a jinking winger to a more orthodox central midfielder, perhaps now we would have called him a holding midfielder or anchor-man. I did score one exceptional goal from around 40 yards out late on in the match. I was too knackered to run the length of the pitch so I tried a speculative strike from the right side of the pitch with the goalkeeper slightly off his line and watched as the ball sailed into the top right corner of the net. Nevertheless, I was dropped for the next match to substitute, then dropped completely.

Grammar school classmate Roger Apted says he has one abiding memory of our lunchtime football matches played in the yard, with balls of various sizes (depending on who was able to bring one in on any particular day and how many we had lost on the flat roof or burst in our enthusiasm to get stuck in):

"One 'event' I remember clearly from Chosen Hill lunchtimes was a goal we scored in the playground football games. We were playing down the slope from the metalwork classroom end towards the main school building. The ball came down the right wing and was crossed towards me in the inside right position. I remember doing an outrageous dummy to mislead the goalie because I knew you were coming in behind me. Everything went perfectly to plan and you duly rocketed the ball into the net (well fence actually}. It was the best goal I participated in during my 6 years of playground football." Roger was the one player everyone wanted on their side when teams were picked so his highest praise is much appreciated.

I do have recollections of trying out for a local team once I left university and started work, but the adventure lasted only until training for the first match had ended, leaving me a crumpled heap of well-intentioned but totally unfit 23-year-old.

Back in Churchdown, we lived at the southern end of the village, which was long and thin. We were at one end of the sausage shape, while the sportsground and public facilities were at the northern end. To begin with, dad cycled to work, taking 11 or so minutes to do the 3 miles to the office. Without a car, it made it difficult to consider taking part in any sporting events. Even the club tennis courts were up in the village proper. Taking public transport to sporting events never seemed right somehow.

My father would have loved me to have been a rugby player. He had played just about every sport in the Fleet Air Arm, excelling as a hockey striker, and as a wing-forward in rugby. He had not surprisingly perhaps won the long jump at sports day too and proudly showed me his winners medal.

On leave from the Navy, dad had been selected to play for his home town's rugby union side in Newbridge, Monmouthshire. They would often become national champions. It had been difficult for him to play rugby at his peak, the war getting in the way! He was married and in his early twenties already, before he was able to play the occasional game during his leave, and then later when he would have been at his absolute best he was on tour of duty in Korea. By the time he left the Navy in 1956 he was already 30, and although he made several star appearances for Cheltenham, he had reached the pinnacle of a career, which, in its brief time, had seen him very near to a Welsh trial.

For my part I carried over some of the skills I had honed in football to the rugby field. I could run with the ball. Fast. I didn't want to get caught, so give me the ball and I would run. Dad bought me a rugby ball and spent countless hours on the green giving me high balls to chase and catch, shouting "Mark" as I caught them. I found playing at the back as a sweeper suited my abilities, dropping on loose balls before rising swiftly to my feet and booting the ball into touch, or running to swoop up grubber kicks before depositing the ball in the crowd. Provided my action didn't take me into direct contact with the opposition I excelled.

When I wasn't selected at full-back I played scrum-half or fly-half, when my speed with the ball would allow me to slip in and out of the opposition's hands, or on the wing. I was pacey enough, but once caught, I tended to lose the ball as it was stripped from my hands. Fast I might have been, but at 9 and a half stone in my stockinged feet I was not the strongest lad in the backs. In fact, in training, having 'missed' a tackle, I would occasionally be called upon to tackle one of the other lads to serve as an example to others, or to be tackled for the same reasons. "Harris, let MacMillan tackle you". I would set off at a fair lick, determined not to allow Mac anywhere near me. This usually backfired as the teacher hauled me back for Mac to have another go. "Too fast, Harris" he would shout. "Let him catch you!"

It was in this way that when heavy frost put paid to proper rugby a certain young winger was able to excel at touch rugby, skipping and jinking through the opposition ranks to score touch down after touch down, bending and swaying to avoid being touched, just like your typical Welsh fly-half.

I therefore was not surprised never to be selected for the firsts. Our school firsts were outstanding, winning just about every match they played and by extreme margins against local public schools drenched in rugby history. Many of the team played for the county, 3 of the team were selected for the winning 'probables' England team against the 'possibles' and subsequently (and mysteriously) left out of the final England team. The names of Cassidy, Taylor (yes! the same one!) and Schultka became iconic in our school history.

There were days when I was on fire, drawing applause from the 'stands', scoring nippy little tries or dropping goals. I would do something amazing before being ripped to shreds by one of the 'big boys'. And my attempts at some other sports saw me pull off similar brilliant efforts before returning to mediocrity.

I would include darts and table-tennis in that group. Always popular at break-time at work. Never a big hitter at the dart board I could be relied upon to hit the occasional 60 but usually kept the score ticking over with a half-crown (two and six, 26). I could also hit the rare top-spin smash in ping-pong but mostly, in spite of building up a good old sweat, I lost. Two sports I really enjoyed, but without real success.

I worshipped Franz Klammer as a young man, his bravado and guts as he flashed down the icy stretches of the Lauberhorn at Wengen, or the Hahnenkamm in Kitzbuhel. We did get a little snow in Churchdown, but never enough to contemplate joining the ranks of the skiing fraternity. I watched in black and white for many years before colour television added to the excitement of the downhill. I did not imagine that one day I too would set off down the Hahnenkamm, but more of that later.

I studied the skiers on tele for many years, enjoying the exploits of Stenmark, Americans Mahre and Johnson, Killy, Tomba, Zurbriggen and Muller. I imagined what it must be like to thunder down the slopes, snow flying in all directions.

So, I booked a holiday in Austria, in Zell am Ziller to be precise. I began squatting and thrusting to build up my core muscles. I took lessons too at Gloucester dry ski slopes. After one such lesson, during which I fell over more times than I care to mention, I set off down the slope in the traditional snowplough beginners stance intended to control your descent. Knees bent, and hands forward, with my poles jutting out behind me, I slid ever so gently down the piste. Now, just to slow down by pushing the back of each ski out and pressing on the inside edges. But, try as I may, the snow-plough stop was failing to slow me down and I accelerated on to the grassy verge and headed for the open doors of the shop. Not a moment too soon, I fell to the ground, split-seconds before I would have zipped across the thresh-hold and (hopefully) back between the door posts into reception and the ski-shop whence I had come minutes earlier! Better to have veered to the right, and crashed, however, than slide off to the left of the piste, with the prospect of the 3 metre drop over into the car park.

What an introduction to the sport!

Zell turned out to be the snowiest town I ever encountered, with roads blocked, cars stuck under 6 feet of the stuff, and white-outs that could have served to define the term. One morning, on a beginner's slope, the snow came down so thick and fast that we were the only ones daft enough to be out. The ticket collector looked snug in his hut, fire on, with a good book. He checked our tickets once before simply waving us through three or four times, until finally ignoring us as we drag-lifted ourselves back up to the top of the slope. Once he had finished his book, he closed up his hut and pushed off home, leaving the slopes to us for as long as we were foolish enough to continue. I went home to England with bronchitis.

Further holidays followed in Ellmau, Gerlos, Saalbach-Hinterglemm, Westendorf and Saas-Fee, among others, as I honed my technique, buying my own boots at Earls Court Ski Show, meeting Konrad Bartelski, the best British skiing had to offer, until I inevitably made the grade anyway.

On one occasion I found myself on a particularly icy piste, traversing far too far to the right, and feeling totally incapable of making a turn. I stopped where I was, unable to launch into the turn because of the steepness of the hill. Just at that moment I spotted help further down the slope in the shape of an instructor, dressed in the traditional all red coat and ski-pants. They could sense I was frozen to the spot, and waved to me, before side stepping up the snowy waste towards me, a good thirty meters higher on the mountain. I watched in admiration as they literally edged towards my position, my poles plunged into the ice beneath my skis to prevent me from slipping.

I was not too ashamed, after all this must happen to beginners all the time. The instructor reached me, and supported me while I took off my skis.

At this point I was advised to walk down the hillside until I reached the bottom of this steep section while she slung my skis over her shoulder and snowploughed them down to where I would eventually join her. Yes, it was a young and extremely skilled *lady* instructor who made me feel an extremely embarrassed fella, on what had been a relatively straight forward red run, and not even one of the more challenging black runs. I have to admit that, without her assistance, I could well have frozen to the spot. I was on the verge of becoming a permanent obstacle.

Then there was the time I leaped on to a chair lift to travel kilometres up the mountain only for one of my skis to fall off within yards of the departure point. All the way up the mountain I worried about how I was going to get down the slope on one ski. In the event, minutes later my ski came up the chair lift accompanied by a bearded lift operator and his handsome dog, who received his reward, of snowballs thrown for him to catch in his mouth as he jumped around in the thick snow.

So, how come I skied the Hahnenkamm? Didn't I say that earlier? Well, yes, I did, and it's true to a degree. I had reached the restaurant at the top of the Hahnenkamm by cable car and before me lay several pistes to choose from, one green, the easiest route, a couple of blues and reds, and a notorious black run, which I was determined to avoid at all costs.

I made my way gingerly down to the blue run, before inadvertently sliding past the blue run marker and over a ridge. With increasing horror, I realised that I had accidentally slipped on to the very top of the black run.

While my legs shook with fear, I scrambled my way back up, on skis and gloves, the three or so yards I had skied down the Hahnenkamm. I could not imagine what delights the mountain would have thrown my way had I not managed to return to the blue run. I did breathe deeply for a few minutes to regain my composure I can tell you.

To be fair, I also skied the bottom of the Hahnenkamm on the beginners' slopes in the village, so I guess I can honestly say I have skied the Hahnenkamm top to bottom!

Skiing is another of those sports that I remain typically average at, the latest experience having been in the French Pyrenees last spring, but many people will never have had the opportunity to try out the sport so I feel myself very fortunate to at least have had a go and to enjoy the experience, not to mention après-ski at all hours of the early morning.

Back on the flat, and turning now to racket sports, which have emerged from time to time in my sporting life, I guess it all began with the front wall of my house in Churchdown, and with the friendly, open-minded Lancastrian Mrs Mac, who lived next door.

I always loved watching tennis. I grew up in an age when tennis was going through huge changes, the Open era was coming of age and players such as Laver, Newcombe and Roche, plus the evergreen Ken Rosewall were dominating world tennis. My wooden racket was purchased with the intention of developing a devastating serve like Mike Sangster, the stalwart of the English game. I practiced serves against our pavement wall, above which we had a thick hedge. The aim was to just clip the top of the wall, about net-high. Of course, a successful serve meant spending countless minutes scrabbling round in the hedge searching for the ball, the harder and more successful the serve, the deeper into the hedge the ball would sneak. A fruitful afternoon's practice usually meant arms covered in scratches, sore, but well worth it.

This low wall was no good for stroke play however.

The house was semi-detached with the door to the left of the front wall with the front room window alongside it. There were two bedrooms, the windows of which were situated precisely above the door and front room window leaving a square of brickwork for me to aim at.

Now, although the front garden was laid to lawn, it was surrounded by a flower patch on all four sides, which made the bounce of the ball unpredictable to say the least, which meant that I was obliged to hit volleys against my target area, alternating between forehands and backhands, becoming more and more difficult to retrieve as the angles became steeper and more awkward. I took so many trips into my neighbour's front garden to fetch wayward shots that Mrs Mac got her husband Hector to cut gaps in the hedge so that I could nip through without having to go through the two gates, bless her. Any balls that caught an edge and flew further afield ran the risk of dropping into Mr and Mrs Jones's garden, an altogether different realm. The Joneses were every kid's biggest nightmares. They despised anyone who entered their kingdom without an invitation, and if you had to retrieve a ball, you did so at your own risk. We tried knocking and asking politely for our ball back, but this manoeuvre regularly failed. We were met with what seemed to our young ears like a wild roar of disapproval, a request to 'get back to where you come from', and to speedily vacate their garden. This seemed particularly funny to me as the Joneses had come from Wales themselves, and if I was going to leave Churchdown, surely, they would, by their own reckoning, have to do likewise?

All of this should have dictated that when I finally took up the game seriously, I would have an immediate advantage over my opponents. In so far as my hand eye co-ordination was concerned it did have benefits. I could see a ball, how it would behave in the air, what spin was being imparted, the flight of the ball. I could anticipate a volley opportunity quicker than just about anyone else. The flaw in the ointment was that I was not used to the ball hitting the ground and coming up towards me. True, I had played in the road with both my mum and with David Smith using the huge concrete slab markings of the road as service line and net, but without being anywhere near a true court size and missing a proper net, it had been nothing more than an approximation of a tennis court.

In reality, the courts at school turned out to be much larger than our concrete slabs in the road outside my house, and not all shots were volleys. Nonetheless, I was still quite a decent player once I had adapted to the bounce of the ball, and every day throughout the summer term I would attach my racket to my bike for the journey to school, wooden racket neatly stored away in its sprung wooden frame to prevent it warping.

School was built around a central playground upon which 4 tennis courts had been designed. There was a slight slope on each from the bus roundabout down to the refectory, and in winter when the nets were down, football matches took over.

In the summer, however, tennis ruled the roost, both racket and hand versions. To play the hand version you used the half court and tramlines within the service lines, and hit the ball with your open palms, no other changes to the rules. This led to utter chaos as dozens of balls in play at any one moment, flew in all directions. Add into this chaos the sight of four young lads trying desperately to get a set of proper tennis played while other pupils wandered across the court idly chatting about last evening's television or making plans for the weekend.

Without exception the foursome would involve Kev, Pete, Andrew, Nigel, Ron and me in some combination or other. Occasional substitutes such as Brian would be called upon in the event of sickness, but, essentially, that was the daily line-up. On days when we couldn't get a court, we would gather on the bus roundabout to play alternative versions of palm tennis.

Getting a court became a game in itself. The big secret lay in being in a classroom close to the bell as lunchtime approached, and being the first to volunteer to ring the bell, then, having set the bell ringing, shoot off into the outside world, or failing that, being the quickest out of class and into the playground to 'nab' a court. Nabbing involved putting a jacket or jumper over the net winder to establish your right to the court for as long as you wanted. Mac had become our current record-holder, mastering the silent sliding of the chair from under his desk to give him the space to sprint for the door within seconds. Just occasionally he would fault start. Mr Utteley would shout the famous words. "That boy! Come back here and stop running".

There were 3 sittings for lunch, so it was quite possible to miss out on a court for the first sitting, and then to hang around a court where the players were likely to vacate for their lunch in 25 minutes time, and come to an agreement that when the current 'tenants' left court they would reserve it for your group. Quite a grounding in negotiating skills.

An hour of frantic tennis with very little in the way of end changes or resting between games, often in jumpers and ties, resulted in four or more youngsters going into lunch dripping with sweat, not so conducive to pleasant intercourse over the dinner table.

You will recall that I failed my father's ambitions for me on the rugby field, and that my own ambitions to play football at a higher level had taken a blow when our school had no facilities for soccer. Now it was time for all my tennis hopes to suffer a blow of their own. Whilst we had the courts at our disposal during breaks and after school hours, playing tennis in lesson time was restricted to the girls, as I well knew from idle moments staring out of the French teacher's room windows overlooking the courts.

The boys? Well of course we played cricket. It was as if they were doing it on purpose! Rugby, cricket and athletics, but not football or tennis. If you didn't or couldn't run there was the choice to go swimming, but if, like me, you were rubbish at cricket there was no alternative.

Until the day of the protest.

To get any changes through, we would have to make a case to the Red. He already knew of my limited capabilities on the cricket pitch. On one particular overcast afternoon I had come into bat against a fast bowler, quaking in my boots, bat wobbling in my gloved hands. I had taken guard, middle and off, and looked down the pitch to where the enemy was steaming in. I survived 6 balls, mainly due to the Red's determination to give me a chance to show my ability. On the second ball I swished wildly at the ball only to get an edge straight to the wicket keeper. Out! "Carry on, Harris" said the Red. One ball zinged past my bat, before I was trapped LBW on the next. "Stay there" came the instructions from an unbelieving teacher, unprepared to accept such ineptitude.

Now that I was finally becoming used to the pace of this red projectile speeding towards my nether regions, the sixth ball I managed to make firm contact with, directing it with aplomb straight to the close in fielder at a short gully. This was too much even for the generosity displayed by the Red during my short innings. I was out, again, and off I strode, sighing with relief.

And, so it came to pass that a few of us disgruntled so-called cricketers decided to sign a petition requesting the institution of tennis in the boys' curriculum. This was a big step, because in the (admittedly short) 9-year history of our school there had been precisely zero previous changes.

We need not have worried. The staff recognised that some people are just not cut out for cricket, and they readily acceded to our wishes. From this small step we asked the teachers to arrange inter-school matches with local schools and the school tennis team was launched.

Compared with the huge and momentous success of our rugby and cricket teams, our limited achievements went under the radar. Nonetheless the team went unbeaten throughout its first year and we celebrated victory over several public schools in Gloucester and surrounding villages including Marling and King's. If my memory serves me well, we even arranged for our teachers to provide us with transport to the away matches. It was at one such away day that we experienced a grass court with its low bounce for the first time. It felt to us that the opposition was somehow cheating, because they seemed used to the fact that the ball failed to reach knee height.

I thoroughly enjoyed our tennis matches, perhaps all the more so because they had been unintended for our curriculum and therefore it seemed more of an individual achievement in having organised and participated in them, not to mention winning them.

Occasionally, and it was sadly only occasionally as a treat, we played badminton in the P.E. lessons when it proved too cold or wet to go outside.

I got to enjoy badminton. It was another racket game where hand eye co-ordination helped enormously. I discovered that I had a deft touch, and that, combined with a swift and deadly smash, meant that I could beat most. I bought a Carlton racket, essential then if you were to be taken seriously at the game. It even came with its own cover, on to which I adhered a welsh badge to give credence to my improving skills.

Off to Swansea University I went, now determined to prove myself worthy at one sport at least.

In Freshers week I bravely sought out the badminton club and signed up. The club met twice a week in a Nissan hut type building, no heating and with neon strip lights, not ideal, but at least it belonged to the club. The neon lights were suspended from the ceiling on long chains which made clearing your own lines a tad difficult if you were to avoid clipping the lights. This wasn't the only danger however. Slight damage to the roof meant that on rainy nights – and there were quite a few in South Wales during the winter months – we had to mop up wet patches on the court every few minutes, making play somewhat risky at times, especially when bowls were placed strategically to catch the drips.

Badminton was not perhaps the most popular of college sports, but it had a committed following. In that first year I do recall the humiliation of coming up against two outstanding players. There must have been a dozen or so of us keen enough to turn up twice a week in the cold, of which four would be chosen to compete for the team. One of our group was a very well-groomed young Asian, always smelling of expensive soaps and sprays. He had all the best equipment, beautifully presented in full length zipped carrying cases. He also brought his own shuttlecocks with him, proper feather ones from China, while the rest of us were happy to use plastic ones. He was so polite too, the loveliest of gentlemen in the old-fashioned sense of the word. Short and stocky, he was exceptionally quick about the court, where his lack of height did not restrict him in the slightest. He could get to everything, high lobs and short dinks. He would form the basis of our four-man team. He turned out to be a real-life prince too, though I never got to call him by his regal name.

Alongside him was a tall angular player from Middlesex. After a few weeks of retrieving or more often picking up his lobs, dinks and smashes I learned that he was actually a regular player for his home county of Middlesex. No wonder I was never getting close to challenging him for supremacy, though as usual I was coming up with the occasional stroke of magic.

I believe he was called Mike or maybe Ian, but what I do know is that he had an infuriating skill on court. I say infuriating because what Mike / Ian would do was swing (early) and miss (deliberately) a smash from the centre of the court, giving you the impression that you had won the point, before waiting for the shuttle to drop below shoulder height and gently flicking it over the net to within a yard or so of the centre line. Infuriating, because he could seemingly do this at will, and equally embarrassing at the same time, because you almost knew it was going to happen but were powerless at spotting it. He was clearly our number one, with Princey at number two, and they made a formidable pairing. I would run them close from time to time, and if the university had put out a second team, I guess I would have been under consideration. Another case of being average.

After university I returned to badminton from time to time, mainly after work in local sports halls for fun, but I never pursued it seriously. Neither did I take up tennis other than as a hobby with the lads in the bank, followed by a cold lager and lime on the journey home. Why did I not pay for lessons? In those days more so than these, tennis was considered the game of the middle and upper classes. Even if my parents had been wealthy enough to send me for lessons my working-class background made it unlikely, if not impossible perhaps, to enter into the refined world of tennis coaching at that time, and it was fully twenty-five years before I felt comfortable enough to sign up for lessons, by which time I had more or less forgotten those early skills honed against my house brickwork.

I continue to play tennis right to this day, though there were many years when I left my wooden rackets stashed away in the wardrobe. Having recovered from a bad bout of glandular fever in my late thirties, I did make a comeback on the tennis courts of Newquay, right out on the headland in the winds and storms coming off the Atlantic. This lasted a couple of years without uprooting any trees, though I did make some firm friends during this period. I also had to contend with, and get used to, playing with carbon fibre rackets! Tennis had moved on and I had been left behind.

Then moving to Sheffield in 2004, I discovered a lovely tennis club nearby, set in beautiful rolling countryside of North Derbyshire, and settled down to social club tennis. I was still pulling up not a single tree, but beginning to enjoy the friendship and camaraderie playing tennis could bring. I joined the committee, helped to organise Great British Tennis Weekends to encourage others to join up, played the odd game for the midweek works league team and lasted one or maybe two rounds of the annual club championships.

Being average had never felt so good or acceptable.

5. ICONIC SPORTSMEN AND WOMEN OF MY ERA

1. ALI

2. JIM CLARK

3. SEB COE

4. ILYA NASTASE

5. TREVOR HOCKEY

6. JESS ENNIS-HILL

7. BOBBY MOORE

8. DAN MARINO

9. STEFFI GRAF

10. KELLY SOTHERTON

11. BARRY JOHN

12. FRANZ KLAMMER

6. I ALMOST PRESENTED THE BREAKFAST SHOW

When I was young and growing up to Radio 1, from about 1967, I used to regularly introduce to anyone who would listen, the songs playing out on the radio, speaking over the introductions by Tony Blackburn and trying, like him, not to crash the vocals. And like us all, I recorded the top forty off the radio, trying to time it so that I didn't include the voice of Alan Freeman, but never quite managing it, so I would always have a 'Number 5' or a 'down from 19' or 'eatles' and 'ny and Cher' to spoil the illusion that I actually had the record in my tape collection.

Tony Blackburn was an early influence on me, with his quick quips, Dog Arnold, and his golden all-time classics. I had, of course, grown up with Radio Luxembourg under the bed covers, pretending to have gone to sleep, whilst listening surreptitiously, either quietly under the sheets, or with my earpiece plugged in. Many a time I had given myself away by singing along with my favourite songs, or accidentally unplugging the earphones at which point the indistinct sounds of Luxembourg would crackle and swoosh sufficient to wake my parents in the bedroom next door.

Radio 1 had then come along at the perfect moment for me, after all I was 15 when it kickstarted my interest in pop music in September 1967. By then of course, the Beatles had largely come and gone, though Brian Matthews had championed their cause on the Light Programme (later Radio 2). The only way to hear the chart music prior to that had been the aforementioned Luxy with 'the Prince' and 'Kid' Jensen, or the Top Forty every Sunday, just before Sing Something Simple. Even then, the charts did not reflect wholly the pop music we all wanted to hear, often featuring the likes of Perry Como, Jim Reeves and Acker Bilk, Ken Dodd and Des O'Connor, whose songs were bearable but not 'our scene'.

I had only just been bought my first record player too, and, as I had no income, had to rely on dad bringing home scratchy old seconds from a friend at work. This is how I received my first four records, the most played being Elvis's 'It's Now or Never' and 'A Poor Man's Son' by the Rocking Berries. I also inherited Fleetwood Mac's 'Albatross' but preferred the 'B' side.

I seem to think the first record I ever bought was 'I Feel Fine' by the Beatles.

Most songs in those days had a distinctive intro, and as my record collection built up, so my voiced introductions got more complex, with the time and chart position thrown in for good measure.

This habit has stayed with me. I cannot help myself talking over the start of records when I am alone in the car, ignoring the likes of Steve Wright and

Ken Bruce. You cannot imagine how useful that skill came to prove when eventually I decided to audition for my local Hospital Radio several years later. Not that I hadn't toyed with the idea of presenting on the radio at university in Swansea. They had their own in-house station and I was sorely tempted to give it a go.

I liked music and I enjoyed a wide and eclectic taste. It was, however, far too challenging for me to approach the programme controller for an audition because I had no real experience other than in my head, didn't understand the notion of broadcasting, with its microphones and faders, and what was more important, was still really shy. No good putting on headphones if you were too scared to say 'Boo' to a goose.

Time passed and other interests and employment took over the mindset.

Until I was late-night shopping in Truro one Christmas. I was in my mid-thirties by now. Strolling through the streets, taking in the atmosphere, I came across an outside broadcast unit and a public address. They were playing seasonal music, and of course I naturally found myself introducing each song as it came on! One or two were shaking buckets and collecting funds for charity, and were wearing sweat-shirts with Hospital Radio printed on them. I got chatting to one of the collectors, found them friendly, and before I knew it, I had a slip of paper with the radio station phone number on it.

Surprisingly, still relatively shy, I made the call, and made an appointment to visit the station one evening. On air that evening was the chairman, and, as it happened, the leading light and top presenter. I was found a seat in what was laughingly called studio 2, the other side of the broadcasting desk, at a small work table.

After half an hour or so my microphone was opened and I was on air myself, only in response to questions fired at me by the presenter, but sufficient to get me involved and to give me a taste of the radio scene. And I loved it. I could not wait to get behind the desk myself. It was during this first experience, that the chairman, in his role as presenter, was asked by a patient to play something nice by the Seekers. Without thinking of the audience, he picked out track 3 on the LP, and out of the speakers drifted the 'Carnival is Over', one of the saddest songs ever. When it got to the part where Judith Durham sings the plaintive line, "I will love you 'til I die" there was a frantic and embarrassed scramble to get the record off air, to the explanation that the record must have been scratched and had to be abandoned.

After the show, I was introduced to my trainer. Ian, although quite young, knew just about all there was to know about the process, the desk, the tape machines, jingles and the record deck.

For a couple of weeks, I sat in with Ian while he produced his own show. Then, he sat with me while I chatted on air – well, to be fair he did more than sit with me, pressing all the buttons, and lining up the records. I learned how far to wind the singles back on the turntable so that when I pressed 'play' they started up promptly without gradually coming up to speed. I found out how to load 'carts' with jingles and adverts. I discovered how to prepare, and listen to, the start of the next song while playing the one on air, by pushing a pre-fade listen (pfl) button. Ian showed me where to place the microphone, the level at which to set the music and speech, and how to open and close the faders.

I will forever be grateful for the unselfish way Ian knuckled down to help me. He turned out to be very knowledgeable about radio in general and charitable in his attitude to others, perhaps, no, certainly, more than the chairman, who was known to hog the limelight and indeed the microphone. This was particularly so at outside broadcasts, and never more so than at the Christmas market. It is perhaps as well that for now his name escapes me, so I am going to call him Dick.

Getting the mike off Dick was difficult. You often had to treat it as a game, offering to say one thing and then hanging on to the microphone. Dick would then put a song on and ask for the mike back.

He thought the world of himself and his presenting skills, but then so did I, well, let's be clear, about me, not him, and, at least, the skills element.

On a Thursday night I would either open up or take over from local dj, Tony Townsend, who went on to appear on commercial radio in Newquay with Atlantic fm. He was a fine broadcaster and we made a good team.

I would call in on my way home from work, and my day was complete whenever I received a message from Tony, that he was stuck at work and couldn't make it, which meant that I could have a double slot. I would drop in at the children's wards first to collect requests either from the letter-box drop if I was in a hurry, or as written requests from the kids themselves while I sat at their bedside.

Some little ones were in hospital for weeks on end, and I got to know them well. One particular lad had been in hospital on more than one occasion and I knew his laugh and his voice. On one particular Thursday, a nurse approached me to say that he had decided not to receive any more treatment and that he was being discharged. He asked me if I would play 'The Eye of the Tiger' for him before he went home. Tears ran down my face when I put the needle on the record and announced his request. I can still visualise that young boy every time I hear the song and bring to mind how brave he was.

Outside broadcasts were by far the most exciting aspect of the 'job', and we provided the p.a. for Lions charity events and carnivals in Truro at Boscawen Park, in Portreath, Newquay and so on. At the time I joined, we had a flimsy tent-like unit within which we would set up a mobile desk, the unit allowing no more than say two persons in at any one time, ideal for Dick of course.

On a fine day, the announcer would venture out of the unit, whereupon a second person would pop inside to play the music. This was OK in theory, except that Dick kept all the 'stuff' at his house, and drove it to the venue. Not ideal. Especially if anyone else wanted to 'have a go'.

Most of the rest of the crew were useful to put up and dismantle the unit and to shake the collecting tins. I detected mutterings right from the start, and after I had been accepted on to the committee felt it was time for a change. I suggested we apply for a grant from the Lottery funding. The committee liked the idea so much they elected me as organiser of the grant application.

Those application forms are enormous you know! Something like 30 pages to complete. Accounts, rules and regulations, charity registration, statement of intent, amount requested, quotes from manufacturers and so on and so on.

I didn't mind in the least, as the £5000 I had put in for would pay for the new broadcast unit in full, a unit which we could tow to any venue we liked, and leave set up with the presenting desk and cd players in situ, and which would allow several members access at once.

Ideal.

Everything in those days was done by letter, and after 7 or so weeks we got our response.....the man from the Lottery, he say 'Yes!'.

Using Yellow Pages, I phoned around for the best deal, not that there were hundreds of them available. With plenty of cash at our disposal I managed to get a brilliant deal, and with a huge fanfare we took delivery of our new OBU (outside broadcast unit).

This immediately put us in a much better place to provide commentary at local events. We would be dry and warm, be able to play cds and make announcements without standing out in all weathers, and provide a more professional service to our users. It also meant that for the first time we would be able to invite guests into the studio for interview rather than expose them to the rigours of the Cornish elements. Moreover, we could park the unit at the Hospital.

Out of the blue, Radio Cornwall contacted me. They had heard about my efforts to obtain the OBU, and wanted to interview me. This would inevitably mean a trip down to the studios with the opportunity to meet the programme controller, and who knows what kind of doors would be opened. If they knew about the OBU, what else had they heard about my show, which had been put up for an award in the annual Hospital Radio Awards. For days I rehearsed my replies to questions about my broadcasting style, my choice of music and features in the show. This was going to prove life-changing, I was certain.

Until I received a phone call that shattered my illusions – Radio Cornwall were on the line, and I was still at work. They wanted to speak to me this morning. Well, I couldn't possibly get to their studios down by the river that quickly could I, and that was what they would want, surely?

It was all OK however, because **they** would come to **me** with a mobile recorder and interview me in one of our offices. My heart sank through two floors to our reception area where it landed with a thud. Hoist on my own petard. They could do outside broadcasts too.

I think it must have been just after the purchase that we attended a country fair near Redruth. I remember that my son Andy had travelled with me and that I entrusted him with my camera for the day. The chairman, Dick, had told us in advance that Sebastian Coe, the famous runner and now local MP would be at the show, and that he was going to try to get an interview with him.

It was a glorious day. The sun was high in the sky and crowds had been building from late morning. We were placed on the fringes of the show ground near the entrance, just right for our collecting tins. Dick was making his way through the crowds with a dapper young man in tow. It was indeed Seb Coe. And up on to the gantry they came.

At that stage we only had one outside broadcast mike switched on, and you can guess who had firm hold of that. Dick introduced the local celeb to the crowd and proceeded to ask the usual mundane questions you might expect. Wasn't this a great turnout, did he like to attend country fairs, what were his hobbies now that he had stopped running. It was good of Mr Coe to stop by and grace us with an interview. By now, I was vice-chairman of the station, and it felt right for me to join Dick and Seb on stage. I motioned that I would like to ask a question myself and Dick handed me the opportunity.

I wanted to know whether he could ever be himself when he was out and about, or did he always have to 'be' a member of parliament. Seb looked surprised, and said what a good question it was. He would have to think about that, and then he gave a considered and well-constructed response which nicely brought his time with us to a close. I had made my mark, and I believe I was taken that little bit more seriously by the team from that point on.

Back in the studio my show was going well. I asked my little girl Rachy to record a smashing little jingle for me. 'Malcolm Harris, he's cool, he's smart, and, what else, daddy?' I recorded my own 'old geeza' introducing the 'Sensational Sounds of the Swinging Sixties' over a segue of 60's intros, recorded on a new-fangled mini disc player at home, from my hundreds of sixties records. Once again, my love of imitation had helped me out.

And I was helped out in the studio by a Steve Wright-like posse of young wannabee presenters in 'studio 2', who also visited the wards and answered the phone.

I negotiated with a local music store for the latest 'Now' album on c.d. to be available for collection more or less on its release date, and was lucky enough to be able to borrow two or three of the latest releases to play on Thursday before swapping them for the following week, thus enabling my show to be up to date with the new release music scene as my younger listeners demanded.

In my role as publicity officer, I took on the production and editorship of a new twice-yearly publication, 'Truro Hospital Radio Is on Air and In Print', seeking out advertising and sponsorship from local shops such as Boots, Dixon's, and C & A.

I was more than happy to put in the extra time and energy if we were to attract further publicity to our charity's activities within and outside the hospital, and I worked hard to make the publication fun and instructive.

The magazine contained pen profiles of the presenters, a competition to win Michael Jackson, and a children's page, together with a radio programme guide to the station's shows. I had obtained a life-size cardboard cut-out of Jacko and offered kids a chance to take him home with them.

The magazine also included a request form. I hoped it would start a regular commitment by the charity to the hospital patients and their families, but I cannot tell you whether another issue ever saw the light of day as I left the county shortly after the production of edition one.

Hospital radio has always been seen as a ready source of radio talent. I was determined to discover how far I could go in the business and so began taping my show from beginning to end, from which I could extract the 'best bits' to submit to local radio stations.

This in itself started to take up a lot of my spare time, cutting and splicing introductions, adverts and interviews on to mini disc. It was not particularly easy to reduce an hour or hour and a half to 3 or 4 minutes. Then to copy to a fresh disc and address it to the local stations including the BBC, with a c.v. and letter of introduction.

I was oh so aware that radio stations must be receiving hundreds of tapes a week, and I knew that unless they had a vacancy they would not be in the market for another presenter, so I had not built up high hopes.

However, I received some encouraging emails, from a Plymouth station, and from Cornwall and Devon's largest commercial station based some 12 miles away in Redruth at Carn Brae.

Plymouth Sound were the first to contact me, inviting me down to their studio for an interview and to sit in on one of the morning programmes. I drove over early one morning and was warmly greeted by a young presenter as if it was all a *fait-accompli* and that I would be joining them, or at least their sister station.

I was seriously flattered that they knew all about me and what I could offer.

Would I like to sit in and shadow the show? They wanted to show me how to set up the adverts, ensuring that no more than one advert of its type occurred in any one slot, one garage, one shop etc. The system they were using was part computer, part presenter driven. When would I be able to start? How long to get from Newquay to Plymouth?

I had set out that morning hoping to make some sort of an impression with the hope that they would put me on a waiting list if a vacancy arose sometime soon, NOT that I would be swept to the top of the leader board! I was just a bit overwhelmed in their faith in my abilities.

And then there was the 50-mile journey to undertake both there and back for what seemed like a poor financial return.

I was beginning to back off, to lose confidence, to find excuses. Could I honestly give up work to commit to an uncertain future?

I had the support of a good woman, but even she was sensible enough to know that finances were going to be an issue.

7. COMMERCIAL RADIO: PIRATE FM

It was while I was mulling the offer over that I received a letter from Pirate FM, undoubtedly the biggest and best commercial radio station around our parts. The letter was from their programme controller thanking me for my tape and praising me for my relaxed style, which I guessed was tongue in cheek, because my style was more cheerful and lively than relaxed. Phil Angell asked me to call in for a chat.

"It's been over twenty years since we first met Mal and a lot of Cotes de Beaune Villages has flowed under the bridge since then," says Phil Angell.

"I joined Pirate in December 1998 so your arrival as a freelancer would have been in 1999. My first thought then about you has stayed with me today - and you'll like it! When I heard you on air I thought 'thank God.' Why? Because frankly Cornwall was not blessed with a plethora of radio talent and finding decent freelancers had proved impossible."

I did just that, I called in by appointment, and was almost immediately brought in as cover for Duncan Warren on his Saturday morning oldies show when he was ill or on holiday. I sat with both gentlemen to learn the ropes, time having moved on, and computers now setting up most of the music and a good number of the adverts. There was still a fair amount of back counting to the news to be done, and links to the travel and traffic, and the football and rugby reports that came in regularly. There were also the station idents to read out, and the weather to read out after the news. I was shown how to bring up the correct interview for the news items, and, in the back office, how to edit the reports coming in off outside agencies. I was so excited – and what's more they were paying me too. Not a huge amount, £25 per show, which I eventually negotiated up to £40, but never enough to consider leaving my day job.

On my first official programme, where I could announce that I was Mal Harris, standing in for Duncan Warren on the 11 o'clock Saturday morning show, I was very nervous, near on bricking it to be fair. I had to be in the studio as soon as the previous presenter had completed the weather and go live after the adverts. My first words are unlikely to go down in showbiz history. I was slightly confused by the time of day, and so blurted out the immortal line, 'Hello, good afternoon, good morning' before introducing the first record programmed into my friendly computer. From then on, I relaxed and stuck rigidly to my script, announcing the chart positions and years of release of the oldies in the schedule that day.

I tried to keep it simple, remembering that we had two transmitters pushing out two separate sets of adverts depending on the area of transmission, and linking with the travel and traffic before the news. On the hour, the news reader would ceremoniously march into the other side of the glass, having handed me a short list of items, each one given a letter of the alphabet, then, having opened their mike, they would point at me to signal the point at which I should hit the aforesaid letter of the alphabet on the machine to my immediate right. This would select the appropriate piece of dialogue for transmission, whether it was a politician, sportsman or spokesman.

Just occasionally the news reader would issue a challenge to me, or, in layman's terms, make a balls-up, by attaching the wrong letter to the wrong item, and John Major's voice would follow an article on a chess championship, or Serena Williams would pop up to discuss the European Space Agency chances of landing a probe on Mars. Whilst this sometimes resulted in much corpsing on our part, there would be a frantic fading of the recording followed by an apology that there had been some sort of a technical issue.

Unlike the regular presenters, with their regular features and competitions, I had nothing prepared for me to say, and so I occasionally resorted to 'things in the press you might have missed' such as the sale of John Lennon's piano. Some guy had bought the piano John Lennon used to write Imagine, not realising that it was not the splendid white grand piano from the film, but an ordinary upright he was buying.

I served an apprenticeship, and over the weeks I became more assured and I found my voice.

109

"You were the only one I found in my two years as Pirate's Programme Director who was both reliable and competent. You didn't sound like someone trying to be a radio presenter; you were a radio presenter. I always dreaded a mainline presenter taking a holiday if it meant a below average presenter replaced them for a fortnight. I used to think listeners would flee in droves. If you did the show though I could sleep better at night!" Phil Angell has very kindly commented.

Like all radio stations the 'swing jocks' as we were known, were used to fill schedules when no-one else fancied them. So, I found myself filling in on 6-hour Friday night shifts, or on a Saturday afternoon between 2 and 6 when the sports results were coming in. Can you guess who was scheduled to do the breakfast show one New Year's Day?

It was funny that morning. I was alone in the studio, no news reports or traffic and travel, just yours truly. The computer sorted out the music and ads, while I was able to fend off the phone calls between the links. After 3 or 4 phone calls to the studio regarding lost animals, which I duly read out in the hope that people recovering from the exploits of New Year's Eve might spot, through bleary eyes, in their front gardens, it occurred to me that I was getting too many of these calls. After all, I had never heard Pirate reading them out before. I reminded listeners that I was 'Mal Harris' and not 'Rolf' who, at the time, was a regular on television vets' shows.

What I discovered later, was a basket labelled 'Lost animals to advise RSPCA' where presenters were supposed to leave appropriate notes to pass on to the authorities, NOT to read them out on air! Even so, I was able to reunite one or two pets with their owners that morning, so all was not lost – literally.

After a while, I moved about the schedules, filling in on the evening show, sometimes for a full week, but more often just on a Friday. The Friday show was just a bit different and lasted the whole evening from 6 til 12. This was a test on many levels. No newsreader to keep me company. Nobody to cover me for bathroom breaks. No travel and traffic presenter. No script. Just me and the computer, so not even the choice of music. If 'Chirpy, chirpy, cheep cheep' was scheduled, that is precisely what I played.

My spell at Pirate taught me many lessons. One was not to 'um' and 'ah' (thanks Phil) unless you meant it. Another, was not to trust any of the other presenters. Jealousy was rife in an unpredictable atmosphere. Duncan was OK, very affable, and he later went to Radio Cornwall. But there was one particular presenter who tried more than once to 'drop me in it', letting the controller believe that I had pre-recorded my tea-time shows when in fact I hadn't, so that there would be empty air when the programme was due to go out. I began to believe in Karma when one Saturday he left the studio with twenty minutes of his show to go and, instead of the next show being primed to begin at 6, it failed to kick in. Silence was certainly not golden that afternoon.

Occasionally, a young child would ring up for an autograph, and on rare occasions a pal from Hospital Radio would call up.

One dark night, approaching midnight, I made my usual rounds of the building, checking doors and windows prior to setting the alarm, locking up the station and going home. As I walked down a corridor at the back of the offices, a door handle moved, the door marked 'fire escape only'. Being alone, there was nobody to ask for advice. I knew I had to keep the programme going and could not be in two places at once. I picked up the phone and hesitatingly rang the police, explaining that I was alone and that I could not leave the studio to investigate.

Within minutes, with the air getting chillier by the second, I could see the welcome flashing blues of a police car, and striding manfully to the window the shape of a person I knew well from Hospital Radio. What was he doing exiting a police car though? Simon was a young presenter I had enjoyed working with on the hospital decks, and yet here he was knocking on the window! I was pleased to see a friendly face, especially when it turned out that Si had joined the ranks of the community police. After he did a turn around the building and pointed to the presence of gypsies and their horses in the field behind the offices as the possible offenders, we chatted away until it was time to put the alarm on and wend my way home. Rarely had I been so pleased to see another HR presenter.

There were two trainees on the books at Pirate FM when I was there. As well as myself, there was a young international middle-distance runner called Neil Caddy. I had seen him on television at the AAA championships. He was fast, and on the verge of great things. Where is that young lad now?

He is programme controller at Pirate. It does make me wonder what I could have achieved if I had committed. I always stepped back into the shadows. Neil had a natural aptitude for technology, just like Ian (afternoon show) Polmear. I was in awe of these technophiles who could throw switches and splice jingles apparently at will. And what they didn't yet know they could learn in a second. I was, and here comes that word again, average, a bit slow at picking something up, but once I had it sussed it really stuck, so well in fact that I could pass the information on to others in a concise and intelligent way.

Phil Angell was good to me, he was patient. He gave me good advice. But he also made me fully aware that people like Neil were single-minded and committed in a way that someone like me with a full-time job could never be unless they were prepared to throw the day job aside and bury themselves in radio 24 hours a day. Neil could and would come in overnight to steer the automated programme, while I was fast asleep in preparation for the banking world. The advantage I had was I had already presented live on air and at outside broadcasts, but he was catching up fast, overtaking me on the back straight, so to speak.

On the grapevine I heard a rumour that Pirate was looking for a breakfast presenter and that my name had been mentioned. You can imagine how I was feeling, and yet, had they offered me the position, would I have had the balls to grasp the nettle? Now, that does sound painful!

Domestically, I was the breadwinner. I did not know whether I could bring home enough bacon (to mix metaphors) to make it work.

Phil Angell again: "Could you have made it in radio? Well, yes. Would it have been the right thing for you? Well, no. It's possible that at the time you lacked the confidence to go full-time but (and again this is from memory so apologies if it's wrong) I felt you had doubts that the radio industry itself could give you the financial security you wanted. In short, your doubts were less about you and more about the sector."

"If I'm right, your instincts were correct. That's why it wouldn't have been the right thing for you. At the time of your freelancing for Pirate, the golden years of radio had ended or were ending. In the years to come competition for people's attention would grow not just from hundreds of additional radio stations but from the internet, streaming, the rise of computer games, digital TV channels, talking books, podcasts etc. The economic model of the Pirate you knew would be and is a busted flush today" continues Phil.

"I'm therefore not sure that had you decided to go full-time, your radio career would have been what you would have hoped for. It could easily have led to redundancy or you having to voice-track a show whilst also helping do sponsorship and promotions or some other non-on-air role. Today, radio freelancers at Pirate's level might get paid £60-£80/shift. On most commercial radio stations outside of the big city stations, virtually all presenters would today earn anything between 18k-25k. Not many radio presenters have mortgages. They can't afford them."

If, and it is a big if, I had really wanted it enough, wouldn't I have made it work? I should have been at the door to the studios hammering to come in, to get more on the job training, to learn all there was to learn, to convince the controller to give me the job. Instead, I sat back and waited to hear.

In the event, Phil was promoted. My guiding light had been extinguished, and in his place came Bob. Bob was not only a controller but an accomplished presenter himself. He was now the prime candidate to take on the breakfast programme himself. He called me in for a chat. And that was that.

He no longer required my services. I had gone from potential breakfast presenter, albeit in my own mind, to nothing, in moments, and I was gutted. I held back the tears as I headed for my car and the 30-minute drive home.

Radio can be a cut-throat business. You appeal to one person, not to the next. When your boss becomes your rival, you stand little or no chance. I should have listened to Phil. If you want something bad enough you tear down walls for it, you beg, steal and borrow, you grovel and you plead. I clearly didn't want it enough. Or perhaps I enjoy saying, 'That could have been me on there. Feel sorry for me because I lost out.' If it can be seen as someone else's fault then maybe it's OK. "How close was I".

Phil's final thoughts are these: "So looking back on the little I know of Mal Harris's career I'd say you reached a crossroads 20 years ago where you saw a sign that said "RADIO" with an arrow pointing to your left. You were tempted. You mulled and mused and dreamt of taking that turn but instead carried on. That was the right call. Radio is still grappling with what it should be in an ever changing 21st century and I really don't think you would want to be in it today."

While all this was happening, another player entered the game. A new local newspaper had sprung up in Newquay, The Newquay Voice. The owner and publisher, a friendly guy called Andy Laming, wanted to build up a bit of a media empire and to include radio within his franchise. From small beginnings with the paper, which may have been free I cannot recall, he intended to add a radio station to his stable and he applied to produce an RSL. Now, an RSL or restricted service licence operates on a low frequency and for a short time only, limited to 28 days consecutive broadcasting.

Newquay is seasonal, with the town growing out of all proportion in the summer months. Malibu Surf FM came about in the late 1990s to coincide with the ever-popular August surfing competitions and the hordes of people who poured into the town for sun and more. Complete with jingles and advertising packages, it aimed to appeal to the young surfer and families on holiday. I picked up a copy of the new paper out of curiosity and read with more than a little interest about the proposed radio station.

I set to work on a demonstration tape and once it was finished popped down to the newspaper offices in central Newquay. The boss liked what he heard, and coupled with my experience on hospital radio, I was pencilled in for a show. Much of what was going to air would be aimed at the dance audience, with reggae, drum and base and 'r and b' well covered. My task would be to appeal to the families on holiday in the resort on a mid-morning 'Info show' with tide-times, surf reports, pop music and news and interviews. I decided to feature a non-stop music half-hour, dedications and an item for the kids, who were invited to spot my Larry the Lamb bleating during the programme and ring in for a prize. Very Tony B don't you think?

Malibu Surf ran for several years, from the back of the watch shop one year, from above a surf shop another year, from the grassy surrounds of the top hotel in town another. I was there whenever I could, weekdays during my 3 weeks summer vacation the first year such was my enthusiasm, weekends when I couldn't. I interviewed local celebrities including politicians and surfers, and generally built up my c.v. just in case a big station came calling. We all had Malibu t-shirts, there were giveaways, parties and competitions and it was seen as a huge success.

Of course, the organisers of Malibu had big ambitions too. It was widely known that in due course there would be opportunities to bid for new radio frequencies in and around Cornwall and Malibu's success would be essential in any bid the team was likely to make. I wanted to be in on that! It might even mean bidding against Pirate FM.

It was an odd sensation being on air with Malibu. One moment you were buried away deep in the heart of Newquay, behind closed doors but very much aware how busy the town was, answering phones and playing

117

requests, the next you emerged into the light and joined the bustling throngs as they pushed and shoved their way through town. You went within seconds from being a voice to many listeners to an anonymous face in the crowd. Part of you wanted to ask whether they were listening to Malibu. Strangely, people still recognised me. They heard my voice in shops or in the bars after a show. Coming up to me, some shaking my hand, they said, wasn't I that bloke on Malibu? The one with the lamb? Wasn't Malibu great! Loved your show.

Malibu came and went each summer and the local radio station was no nearer fruition. When we moved out of Cornwall in 2004, I left my name with the Newquay Voice and thought no more about it. I understand that Radio Newquay has launched this year, 2018, and I wish it all the success in the world. Inevitably there are still people I know presenting in Cornwall, such as Tony Townsend, Duncan Warren and James Martin, who followed me from Hospital Radio into Pirate FM.

There ought perhaps to be another sub-title here at this point. 'Side effects' maybe.

You see, presenting on Pirate FM enabled me to add several other arrows to my bow, arrows that would come in handy in the most unexpected of circumstances later in life.

My wife, Denise, was working as receptionist in a Newquay hotel. I used to drive her home and bump into the owners, Ian and Lesley, from time to time, on foot rather than running them over, you understand. Ian had been a commercial pilot, regularly flying the route to Ireland, and he took great pleasure in regaling me with stories primed to fuel my intense dislike of flying, though to be honest, once I had taken into account the unlikelihood of his tales of woe ever recurring, the more relaxed and at ease I felt on my holiday flights abroad! His wife Lesley on the other hand had been a child star on early television. She appeared on Junior Showtime with Bobby Bennett and Mark Curry, and so was thrilled when I said that I could recall some of her programmes from my youth. They made a lovely couple, and I am pleased that they remain my good friends.

It was one of those hotels that welcomed coachloads more than cars it would be fair to say, and in the high season of summer and Christmas attracted tourists with reduced price packages to include food and entertainment, not specifically, but mostly, aimed at senior citizens intent on a good time. Most nights there would be a quiz or bingo, and one evening Den said that the boss was fed up with doing the bingo calling every night and would welcome a break. Had I thought about filling in for him now and again?

To be honest, no, I had not. I was already working full time, and doing the odd shift at Pirate, and that was probably enough to be honest.

Needless to say, the following week I was at the hotel just after dinner calling out the numbers, complete with two fat ladies. Not content with that, I was roped in to perform a quiz the next week, and before I knew it, I was the regular entertainment host. I held 'common denominator' quizzes,

119

'Who wants to be a winner of a box of chocolates', 'Ones and twos' where guests were asked to move into circles marked out on the dance floor to select whether a song had been number one or two in the charts, eliminating the wrong-uns until only one player was left, 'Play your Cards Right' with giant cards and a home-made board, and oldies discos using the superb house p.a. system.

My 12-year-old daughter Rachy was 'pencil girl' handing out stationery and collecting quiz answers, while my wife helped with handing out prizes provided by the hotel, and relaxed with the boss after her shift on reception, while Tanya was busy behind the bar.

We met some lovely people, especially during turkey and tinsel weeks, and got to know returning guests – well, they seemed to remember us. It was sometimes a case of hugging someone while at the same time racking your brain to see if you could remember them, without them telling you their names. It didn't always work.

Soon, my evenings were filling up such that it was nice to have an evening off from the radio or the hotel.

The undoubted highlight was our 60s disco on December 31st 1999, which went on into the wee small hours of January 1st 2000, with colleagues from my (proper) work joining the coachloads celebrating the New Year. I managed to jump down from deejaying long enough to welcome in the New Year, before returning to playing all the best dance songs the Sixties had to offer. Everyone was up dancing, many in fancy dress, and in spite of the dire warnings we had received about the effect the date change would bring to our computer systems, there was no disruption to the c.d. decks or mikes.

On other nights the aerials controlling the roving mike would pick up the sound of local taxi-drivers reporting back to their office, which made for an opportunity to ad lib. As did the appearance on some occasions of Ethel, who would sit beside me on the stage, listening intently to all I had to say, and mimicking me to the amusement of my audience. "Shall we play a quiz, everyone". Ethel also liked to sit at reception repeatedly imitating the sound of the fax machine, and setting the photocopier machine off with a "Wheeee!".

Ethel was a parrot.

As if I hadn't taken on enough, my daughter had commenced dancing as a weekend hobby for the second time and was enjoying the exercise and companionship of being with other girls of her age. The first attempt had been aborted when floods of tears threatened to disrupt the peace of a Saturday morning trip to school for lessons. She was too young and it proved too stressful. Second time around however, Rachael loved it, took exams, and danced her street dance individually and in team competitions all over the South West, driven to them by her dad, who was also driven, but to distraction by the boom-boom of the loud disco music.

I was the proud owner of a mini-disc recorder, which I used to record jingles for my radio shows, and it came in handy when I was volunteered to produce short segued pieces of music for the teams to perform to. A snippet of Michael Jackson here, some Madonna there, a horn solo from this track, spoken words from another, all spliced and pasted to run smoothly so that, as Morecombe would have put it, 'You can't see the joins!'

'Funky Feet' was more than capable of holding its own against any competition, and ultimately won a place in a show dance at Sadler's Wells in London, and then subsequently at the Royal Albert Hall, dancing to my mini disc, and attended by proud family members and friends, including me and my wife. The comperes were Bonnie Langford and Mark Curry, he of Lesley's Junior Showtime fame. Our hearts swelled with pride.

On their triumphant return to Cornwall, I was invited to co-host a 2 hour show at the Hall for Cornwall in Truro to demonstrate their wonderful talents, and to celebrate with their families and the Funky Feet dance instructor. I was nervous, but at least managed to get through it without resorting to a snifter during the performance, which my co-host kept to hand in the wings! Red wine with ice no less.

It was a great time for me and for my self-confidence, presenting auctions, race-nights, a children's charity disco at Bertie's Night Club in Newquay, and generally helping out at charity events.

You would think that with all that was happening, I could, and probably should, have made it count, used it to bolster my efforts to break into radio full time. My sworn ambition had been to earn my living from something I enjoyed, and yet, for some reason, when push came to the proverbial shove, I sat back and rested firmly on the laurels I had achieved. Does that reveal a flaw in my constitution? Am I the sort of person who is happier saying I could have been this or done that, rather than giving it 100% to achieve one goal? Am I scared either of failing or of being found out?

My involvement with radio did not end with our move to Sheffield.

Somehow, I still fancied myself on the air sufficient to apply for a slot with Sheffield Hospital Radio, and after going through the usual checks and forms, found myself working the Monday night request show before moving to a Tuesday, 8 til 10 o'clock, on a similar request programme. I worked in tandem with other presenters at first, taking it in turns to present, sitting in on the Friday night football show, predicting scores in the local footy matches.

From that I moved on to presenting my own show with co-presenters, usually John and Rachel, or later on, Anna and Simon, and to launching a World Music hour, again with Anna, a delightful young Finish girl, complete with songs from Africa, Australia, USA, the Caribbean and the far East.

In fact, it was Anna, now resident in Northern Ireland, who recently reminded me about an experience which in all honesty I should never have forgotten. It is more likely that, having had the experience, I pushed it right to the back of my mind.

Our studio was on floor T of the hospital block, alphabetically working from A in the basement. If I tell you that the lifts only went as far as floor P, you will readily understand, that by the time you walked the remaining flights of stairs to the studio you were struggling in rarefied atmosphere, particularly if (like me) you were carrying your work bag, coat, and box of cds.

Because we were up in the gods, there were all sorts of rules, including one which said you HAD to enter the studio in twos, just in case of mishaps or sudden illness. One of the other rules was that you were obliged to undertake a fire escape practice.

You may never have climbed Mt Everest, and certainly not I, but one can begin to understand the difficulties involved in such an assault having been guided by my own Hospital Sherpa over the rooftops of Hallamshire Hospital. One late afternoon, light fading, Sherpa marched us out of our office environment into the boiler space at the top of the 20 or so storey building. From here we were led outside on to iron stairways and up on to the roof of the building. In a scene reminiscent of something from Bond or Bourne, we crept across the roof, ducking to avoid central heating ducts and metal bars, walking gingerly on damp flooring, afraid to look down. After what seemed like an eternity, we finally clambered down another staircase back into the building on the opposite side of the hospital. As Anna said to me as I began the writing process, it would have perhaps been safer and much less frightening, to have faced the fire itself.

I was advised to use the computer to schedule my music, but as the music scheduled was largely toothless and tedious, I decided to add my

Sensational Sounds of the Swinging Sixties to the schedule, and feature the story of early soul music.

To spice up my show further I decided to seek out requests from 'celebrities' either nationally famous or from locals such as nurses and doctors in the hospital. It was during this time that I contacted Sheffield Theatres with the concept of reviewing shows in the 2 local theatres. They were only too pleased to add my name to those of local media groups in print and on-line for special treatment: tickets for productions, plays and musicals, and intermission drinks and snacks. I would see the production on a Monday evening and announce my review the following day on air in time for patients returning home to catch the performance by the weekend.

For my celebrity choice, which I nicknamed 'guest request' to cover all eventualities, to begin with I wrote to a couple of Eastenders stars to ask them what kind of music they enjoyed and for them to select a piece of music that I could play for the listeners. Lacey Turner, who I consider one of our finest actresses, was one who kindly replied. This got me thinking. Who was to say that I wasn't just making these requests up?

If I was to be convincing, I had to go one step further and arrange an interview with my celebrity. It was late April and the snooker circus had come to town. Maybe if I hung around the theatre back door, I would be able to get a quick interview. I set off, recorder in hand. At the back door I got chatting with a lovely BBC man. I explained what I had in mind. He thought it was a super idea and he promised to do what he could to perhaps get me a referee to chat to.

Five minutes later and he was back wondering whether Steve Davis, the 5 times world snooker champion would be OK? You will not need me to tell you what my reaction was. Steve Davis, Mr Interesting, was always a hero of mine. I had watched snooker on television since the days when the commentator had found it necessary to describe the colour of the ball being potted, for those of us watching in black and white. With his steady and precise potting and skilful safety Steve Davis was almost unbeatable, especially when the world crown was at stake.

So, I 'made do' with an interview with Steve Davis in the press room of the Crucible. If I could tempt him to tell me what kind of music he liked and pick one track to play I would be happy.

'Come on then, let's get started!' said Steve, and several questions later and nine and a half minutes in, Steve had told me about his latest match against Ding, his opinion on calling yourself a foul shot, his delight at how Sheffield had changed for the better, his soul radio show, and picked no less than three tracks to play on the show. A lovely man, true to his word, and fun to interview. He selected an Aretha Franklin track and anything by Curtis Mayfield, 'but not Move on Up' because everyone always plays the same song by Curtis.

In future weeks I was able to use my new-found confidence to chat to more celebrities at the Crucible and the Lyceum. Waiting at the back door to the Crucible I hijacked Peter Ebdon as he arrived in his chauffeured limousine. "Malcolm Harris, Hospital Radio, Peter" I bravely started. "How are you this lunchtime?" He was well, and looking forward to his match. Was he confident? Did he have a message for all his fans that were currently in hospital? He did, and he wished them all well. I wished him luck. He made the final that year.

Chloe Newsome, Corrie actress, chatted to me backstage. Sitting in her dressing gown she told me how she was living back home for the duration of her Agatha Christie play and being dropped in on the dual carriageway before, and being picked up from the pub after, performances. She dropped the name of her boyfriend into proceedings, whilst telling me that before the cast made up, the girls always sang Oasis's 'She's Electric' to get psyched up for the performance.

Darren Day treated me like a long-lost brother, hugging me time after time, and picking out an Elvis track.

Gerard Murphy, fabulous actor appearing at Sheffield's Crucible to play Salieri in 'Amadeus', appropriately enough chose a piece by Mozart, 'Cosi fan Tutte'.

Snooker ace Nigel Bond, World Championship finalist in the 90s, spoke with passion about the National Health Service and the care and commitment taken in respect of his ailing son, enjoying music in the car on his way to tournaments, while local artist Pete McKee, born in the year England last won the World Cup, surprised me with his choice of music, and spoke with pride about his favourite football team, Sheffield Wednesday. Intending to tape a two-minute chat, Pete and I were still talking 8 minutes later.

One idea that occurred to me was to kill four birds with the same proverbial stone when the X Factor team visited a local location such as Sheffield or Leeds. It was with this in mind, that I contacted Lucy in the X Factor office in London, with the proposal that I would briefly interview each of the four judges, including Simon Cowell, before one of their recording sessions, to sound them out about their particular favourite songs. Lucy explained that the judges generally only turned up at the second audition, once numbers had been reduced significantly after the first audition. This meant that my fab four would not be attending the first session and that in order to ensure my presence at the second audition, I would necessarily have to go through the qualifying process. In other words, I would have to audition myself if I wanted to guarantee meeting them! I have always been able to hold a tune, and love an occasional karaoke, but X Factor?

I entered, and waited.

In this particular year the venue was to be Elland Road football stadium in Leeds, and not Sheffield City Hall as it had been the previous occasion. This meant a bit of extra planning, and with my wife's blessing, a day off work to travel to Leeds. I decided to train it.

I was just a little surprised that my taxi-driver had to set his sat-nav to locate Elland Road, and the trip took longer than I expected. When I arrived at the ground, the car park area was full of people, mostly younger than me, and all of them edgy and excited.

Notices around the ground indicated the starting times and instructed us where to go to sign up and register. I wasn't sure why, but I was nervous. After all it didn't matter whether I got through or not from a singing point of view.

As watching the programme had led me to expect, there were some strange outfits, mini-skirts dominated, while some were clad in uniforms, others in fancy dress.

At the due hour the doors opened, and after registration on the ground floor we were led up to the main gallery where greats of the Football Club graced all four walls. Billy Bremner, Welsh goalkeeper Gary Sprake, Peter Lorimer and 'Sniffer' Allan Clarke gazed down upon us.

I recognised almost all of these fabulous stars from their days of combat with Trevor, and recalled the day I had listened to the '73 cup final on my radio as Nick and I travelled through Normandy, losing signal, and then hearing about the moment the Leeds fans had been silenced by an unexpected Sunderland goal.

Looking around the room I couldn't help but notice how much younger everyone was than me except for one elderly gentleman dressed in a suit. He was attracting attention from the production team, who were using the time to encourage us to participate in one-to-one interviews, which they said would increase the likelihood of our being included in the televised show line-up.

Some of the more outgoing of us leapt at the opportunity. On lad came dressed as a naval officer and he was particularly disturbed to learn that the judges were not going to be present today, and that if you were given a green ticket through to the formal auditions later that month, you would have to ensure you were wearing exactly the same clothes for continuity purposes. This would allow the production team to pretend that there was just the one seem-less audition at which all of us would sing for the judging panel. I, for one, did not volunteer.

In truth a large proportion of the thousands of those taking part would be eliminated well before the televised audition, though the programme still gave the impression that we had all gone through the process.

In small groups we were asked to sit outside the door to smaller offices where, inside, a couple of production team juniors waited behind their desks to listen to our efforts.

The girl in front of me sang like an angel, looked like an angel and when she emerged without the magic ticket, I think I knew my fate before I even went in.

I stood on my mark some 5 yards from the desk. They asked me why I was there. I didn't dare tell them the real reason, so I concocted something about always enjoying singing at karaoke and wanting to test myself against others, before croaking my version of a Neil Diamond classic.

Thank you, they said.

They quietly discussed my performance and politely declined my further participation in the X Factor process.

I had been neither good enough, nor cringingly poor enough to qualify for the 'live' auditions. Clearly, some had been chosen for their back-stories, some for their dress sense or lack of it, others, far fewer in number, for their vocals.

There was no-one available to discuss my interview demands, and so I slinked off to get my taxi back to the station.

XXXXXXXXXXXXXXXXXXXXXXXXXXXXXXXXXXXXXXXXXXXXXXXXXXXXXXXXXXXX

My intention was to interview guests from the sporting world locally too, and I had considered approaching the local football teams to include one or two well-known players to kick off with.

I also intended to ask Sheffield's Jess Ennis to take part in the programme too. I read an article in a free local arts mag, about an athletics coach who was seeking sponsorship for an up-and-coming pentathlete in Sheffield. Her potential was enormous. I was intrigued enough to cut out the article and refer it to the finance director at the company I worked for.

The idea was that our company would see the potential of sponsoring Jess, while I would get my guest request interview for hospital radio. Coincidentally one of our receptionists knew of Jess through a family connection and was sure that she could arrange something for me.

Before long I was in regular contact with Jess's agent, Jonathan, by email, expressing the hope that very soon we could secure funding for her in her efforts to take on the best talent Europe could offer. Jon for his part was sure that Jess would be only too pleased to do an interview for HRS.

It was taking far longer than I had anticipated, but Jonathan was patient, and I remained hopeful.

One day, an email came around, announcing an exciting sporting tie-up.

This was it evidently. We had agreed to sponsor the Sheffield Eagles, the local ice-hockey team, for a year. My heart sank, not simply because now I would lose one of my 'guests', but because they had failed to recognise the huge opportunities that a link with young Jess could bring. I wonder if the hierarchy realised what an opportunity they missed.

I did get to interview Simon MacCorkindale, not so long before his sad passing, and he thrilled both me and my listeners with his passion and admiration for the classics.

Gary Wilmot, best remembered perhaps for his 'Me and my Girl' was a delightful fellow, telling me all about his singing career and his forthcoming album, as well as his efforts to make everyone laugh during his school days. Something rang a faint bell.

At Christmas one year, I met the cast of the Lyceum panto, and spent time with 'Toady' from Neighbours, who loved the Killers, Emmerdale's Hayley Tammadon, an Oldies lover (and incidentally a huge fan of the wonderful Beverly Knight), who picked 2 pieces of upbeat music to 'cheer folk in hospital up', and Sheffield's own top comic Bobby Knutt, born Robert Wass in 1945.

What I had never realised was that Bobby was a top-class guitarist, featuring his playing of Shadows' songs in his Atlantic cruise cabaret act. Needless to say, he chose 'Wonderful Land'.

Oddly enough until I did my research for the interview, I had never realised that Bobby was husband to Donna Hartley. To my mind they made the quintessential odd-couple, but were, by Bobby's own admission, as happy as Larry. (Anyone know who this Larry was?)

One of my final interviews was with a svelte-looking Jayne MacDonald prior to her City Hall performance. Before she chose a Josh Groban classic, she talked about her eclectic love of music, displaying her love of 70s music before a night out, and to her credit was surprised when, after a few minutes, I thanked her and asked her to wrap it up, as she had more than satisfied the brief.

I have the distinct feeling she thoroughly enjoyed the experience of being interviewed by a hospital radio presenter without the usual pressures.

I was keen to make my shows as happy and carefree as I could possibly do. With this in mind I launched what I thought were humorous items such as 'name the star', where I 'showed' the listeners pictures of 4 celebs and asked them to identify them, the 'answers to last week's quiz' (the questions to which had never been aired) and 'just why do we say that?' an item about well-known sayings and expressions with an explanation of their origins.

One such saying was 'his name is mud' and it relates to a doctor by that name (Mudd) who was implicated in the assassination of Abraham Lincoln because he innocently attended to his murderer John Wilkes Booth, when he sought out his help with the broken leg he sustained during his escape on horseback. In hindsight, maybe we should have asked in this feature, who Larry was!

Funnily enough, only one person ever asked me why he hadn't heard the questions to the quiz the previous week!

Finishing my show at 10 at night meant travelling home on the 10.08 tram, so by the time I got back to my wife, chilled, and calmed down, had a bite to eat and got to bed, it was late, and with work early the next morning the show gradually took its toll, and I reluctantly decided to give hospital radio up.

It was not a decision made overnight, but after much soul-searching it seemed the right thing to do to maintain a good work/life balance, something that I had failed to do some years before.

There are days when I yearn to be back 'on the desk' but I still introduce songs as they play out on the radio, though it is now on Radio 2, rather than its big brother on 1!

8. MY TOP TEN DISCS

The Sun Ain't Gonna Shine Any More THE WALKER BROTHERS

Let's Stay Together AL GREEN

Nutbush City Limits IKE AND TINA TURNER

I Saw Her Standing There THE BEATLES

Rock and Roll (I gave you all the best years) KEVIN JOHNSON

Everyday Hurts SAD CAFÉ

Never Let Her Slip Away ANDREW GOLD

Can't Get Enough (Of Your Love) BAD COMPANY

You Can Call Me Al   PAUL SIMON

Almost anything by OLIVIA NEWTON-JOHN

Clockwise from top left: On the mike at Truro Hospital Radio; With the Thursday night team; Providing public address on the outside broadcast unit; Quiz night at the hotel.

The invitation from Phil Angell to meet up at Pirate FM

1st November 1999

Malcolm Harris

Dear Malcolm

Many thanks for your recent demo tape. I was impressed with your relaxing style!

Please call me during office hours on 01209 314400. I would like to meet you to discuss your work to date, and any possible future opportunities.

Regards

Above: waiting for my turn to pose the killer question to Sebastian Coe.

Radio Cornwall interview me about the Lottery award and the purchase of THR outside broadcast unit.

How the press broke the news of my own big break.

Pirate radio break for DJ Malcolm

A BUDDING DJ from Newquay has just moved a step closer to his goal by landing a job with local radio station Pirate FM.

Malcolm Harris, right, who works for a local council, has been interested in radio for a long time and does a spot on hospital radio at the Royal Cornwall Hospital, Treliske.

But last summer he did a regular spot on Malibu Surf FM and his success prompted him to send a tape to Pirate, who, impressed with the sound of his voice, have taken him on as a freelance guest DJ.

Malcolm has always been interested in radio, and for the last seven years, has had a regular Thursday evening show on Treliske's hospital station. But this summer, he saw an advert in the

Cornish Guardian which interested him.

A new radio station for Newquay, Malibu Surf FM, was advertising for DJs. Spurred on by achieving

the runner-up spot in a DJ competition, Malcolm decided to apply and ended up doing a morning show for them.

He then sent a tape of a show he did for Malibu to Pirate FM, who rang and asked to see him. Following an interview, he is now doing shows for them on a freelance basis, covering holidays etc.

Pirate's controller of programming, Phil Angell, says he received about 10 tapes every week and most are not up to scratch, but when he heard Malcolm's voice, he had no hesitation in inviting him for an interview.

Malcolm is still learning the ropes, but has done some programmes already and has high hopes for the future: "I do not have

a regular spot at the moment, but hopefully that is the next step and I am working towards it."

Malcolm is grateful to Malibu FM, which got things moving for him and hopes eventually to make radio a full-time career, although he says at 47, it has come later in life than he expected!

He described his first experience with Pirate as 'nervewracking', but says it is not so bad once he got into it. He has obviously made an impressive start, though, as Phil says if he had a full-time job available, he would probably offer it to him.

Malibu Surf FM will be returning to the airwaves next summer from July 20-August 18.

138

9. I ALMOST APPEARED ON CORONATION STREET

The chapter title could have read, "I nearly appeared on Eastenders" or indeed any t.v. series to be honest. And it isn't so far-fetched as it may initially seem.

As a child I was always an entertainer. I recall singing in a fiercely strong welsh accent into one of the first tape-recorders bought by Uncle Cyril. "In a cottage in a wood a little deer at the window stood. Saw a rabbit running by, knocking at the door. Help me, help me, help me he said, lest the hunter shoot me dead. Come little rabbit stay with me, happy we shall be."

On the recording, now preserved on rarely played cassette, just as the singing voice is unmistakably welsh, so is the pitch nigh on perfect. I loved to sing, and just about anyone would do as an audience. Nans were always the favourites because they never sought to criticise and were almost always thrilled to be picked out. I sang to them, and did impressions, the first I can remember being that of parrot-face comedian Freddie Davies. "I thay" I would spray the words at nan, with a hat pulled down over my ears in a direct copy of that lovely funny-man's catchphrase. I also imitated Harry Worth, "I don't know why, but there it is". And Jimmy Clitheroe off the radio. Plus, later, Frank Spencer. My nans would of course corpse in response.

In the real world I suppose I was probably never quite that funny, but it got me started on the road to the world of entertainment.

Talking in class got me into trouble from time to time at junior school. It also led to my performing at Cheltenham Town Hall!

Mr Davis was auditioning for singers to perform with a combined schools' choir in a concert. One by one he was pulling us out to sing a little something in front of class. He caught me chatting away to David Lowe, probably about football. I would be next. Let everyone see what I had to offer, teacher said. Looking sheepish, I made the short journey to the front of the class and turned to face my peers. I looked at everyone staring back at me and all of a sudden 30 nans peered through the haze of my nerves. This was going to be fun. I sang my sweet ditty and waited for nan to react. They applauded warmly, and the teacher was suitably impressed. I was in.

I have fond memories of standing inches from the giant organ in Cheltenham Town Hall right at the back of the choir and high above the rest, singing songs from European classical composers including 'The Trout' by Schubert. Family and friends were in the crowd, and the performance, with good pals from class, made me proud, and gave me warm feelings inside.

I wanted to repeat those warm feelings. And grammar school provided me with the opportunity to do just that.

Every spring the house system dictated that there would be a short play contest on the main stage. It was open to year 4 pupils who would not be encumbered with "O" levels. Perfect. Auditions took place and I put my name in the hat. I auditioned for the two lead parts in 'The Monkey's Paw', and much to my surprise got the part of Sergeant-Major Morris. For the part I adopted the gruff voice one always associates with that of the square-bashing sergeant-major and my throat suffered for my art in a big way. Think Tudor "Shut up" Williams of 'It Ain't Half Hot'.

My pals Nigel and Jane 'starred' alongside me, and we thoroughly enjoyed the lark of learning lines, rehearsing and performing, both in break time and of course during class-time. Bonus!

Another Carne house actor, Ron Sims, remembers the dramatic moment the mother throws the paw (played by a rabbit's foot) into the roaring fire, only for it to bounce off the hand painted coals and fly into the front row of the audience, causing much riotous laughter 'from those anxious to avoid its baleful influence and those trying to get a memento of Carne's legacy to theatrical posterity'.

The judgment came the following day, with the cast on stage for the English teacher to give his opinion on our acting abilities. We came a valiant third if I remember correctly, though I was happy that my accent was praised, if my baton twirling had at times been distracting, I think he said. By now I had caught the bug and was hooked, if I am allowed to mix my metaphors.

141

I still hadn't got over the sickness when I went to university and took minor roles in French Society dramas, again huge fun and highly sociable events. I have pictures in my cupboard still of my role as a letter-reading policeman, which consisted of walking on stage, legs trembling, hands shaking, to read a letter out to the cast and audience about the death of one of the other cast members. I do know that it was a modern interpretation of a classic play, but other than my role in it I must admit to being mostly in the dark.

I guess I was in my mid to late twenties, when I came down with another bout of theatre fever. I am not altogether certain what prompted it. I was not entirely happy with my career at the time, even though I had been promoted to a position with a bank in Swindon. I was now married. Whether this was a suggestion my wife made, possibly to get me out of the house and from under her heels I do not know, but it would in retrospect make some sense. We both worked for the same organisation and evenings would certainly have been spent talking shop.

How did I find out about the Joliffe Theatre Company? Maybe I saw a leaflet at the Wyvern Theatre when we attended a play or music event there, after all most of the rehearsals took place in a top-floor spare room at the theatre, (until they found asbestos in the ceiling and roof-space and we had to vacate) so it was quite possible the group left leaflets in reception.

What I distinctly remember however is my first read-through in that top-floor rehearsal room. We were seated in a semi-circle, and just like in the movies we were handed a script and asked to take it in turns to read different characters. One of these characters was American. I only knew one American accent, a vaguely Italian American from New York, and I gave it my best shot. I thought it had gone fairly well, after all nobody had laughed at the accent, just the humorous lines I had to read. The audition lasted about an hour and we were told to expect a call. Thank you for coming.

I waited. Days went by and there was no call about my American tour-de-force.

And then one day the house phone rang. And they were offering me a part in a play. No, not the tough talking American guy, but a dithering, pottering, wimpish fellow called Peregrine Potter in a play about a will, a comedy called 'A Tomb with a View'. I didn't know what to think, nor indeed what to expect. The cast were called together to meet the director Kate Goodall and to start rehearsals. There were things to learn right from the start. Where to stand so as not to block other cast members, what it meant to block out the moves on stage, two entirely different things apparently. Where stage left and right were, and how to travel up stage and down. When the director shouted, 'Strike' it did not mean to down tools, but simply to remove items from the stage to prepare for the next scene. It was fascinating, absolutely riveting.

At that early stage (no pun intended) I was unaware that our play was not to be performed on the main Swindon stage at the Wyvern, after all the rehearsals took place there. Several weeks into rehearsals however we transferred to a lovely little theatre in Devizes Road. The Arts Centre became my acting home for years to come, and it was, and probably still is, a delight. Just two hundred seats in the auditorium, with a downstairs area that acted as rehearsal room, coffee bar, drinks and party room, two or three heated changing rooms cum dressing rooms, one for the lads, the second for the lasses. Just enough room for one or two vehicles to bring in much needed props, and close enough to the public car-park where we could park the car for free after 7pm.

'A Tomb with a View' was a financial success, selling out on the three nights (including 5th November 1983) we performed it. Critically, the local paper reported that 'fielding a new team, the company romps through this comedy thriller' and that 'there are engaging performances by Malcolm Harris and Lucille O'Flanagan who have a nice sense of comedy.'

That one line in the evening paper was all I needed to confirm that I had a future of some sort in the theatre world, and I was determined to audition again as soon as an opportunity arose. As it happened, that opportunity would be sooner than I imagined.

The Joliffe Company entered the Swindon One Act play festival and I was fortunate enough to get a part in a short play called 'Ritual for Dolls'. My part was challenging to say the least, and somewhat controversial, because I was playing a toy golliwog alongside a tin soldier, a doll and a drumming monkey. For the part I had to be blacked up and to wear a curly black wig, white trousers, red jacket and a union jack waistcoat. The make-up took ages to apply and even longer to remove. I swear some of it is still lodged behind my ears to this day.

The dolls 'live' in an attic and every night awake to re-enact the lives of the sister and brother who once owned them.

The adjudicator was a chap called Peter English, and I recall that Peter shortlisted me for best actor whilst saying with a wry smile about my accent that it showed signs of wandering from the Caribbean across the Atlantic to Southern Ireland. The company was awarded the first ever best 'entry reflecting the art of production' for the 'ease with which the dolls moved to people and back'.

What happened next was that I went to my wife's hairdressers for a perm. Well, maybe not next, but soon, because I had auditioned for a part in Billy Liar and impressively had been rewarded with the eponymous title role. At the age of 32, I was going to be playing the role of Billy Liar in his late teens. Thankfully I had retained my youthful looks, but my receding hairline was going to be hard to hide. The only course of action was to have a permanent wave, as nan would have said. A play where I would have to act with three girlfriends. Oh, the difficulties theatre land can throw at you.

Billy represented my biggest challenge yet. As the title character I would be on stage practically the whole time. My part was more than twice the length of that of any other character in the play and it took a lot of learning, reading it at every spare moment of the day, evening and night.

The part was also much deeper than anything I had ever played, the character more complex and well-rounded, deliriously ambitious and yet scared, emotionally scarred and internally damaged. It was a part that would really test my acting abilities to the full. I was excited to be chosen as Billy Fisher, but would I live up to the billing of this undertaker's clerk living his life in dreams, never certain whether he was in reality or fiction. I needed to be at once clown and dancer, bugle player and world war two pilot, engaged to 3 girls simultaneously, a true test of my skills and my serious acting too.

Billy Liar was a dream for any 'young' actor, amateur or professional. It allowed an actor to show off almost every aspect of his capabilities, funny, moving, dramatic. I thought the part had been written for me and I was in my element. I walked the tightrope along the front of the stage, I fought off Messerschmitt planes as they attacked me in the lounge, played an imaginary bugle at the going down of the sun and spun around on Sunday Night at the Palladium's stage waving to my fans as I span.

The cast was, as a whole, solid, the reaction of the audience even more special than we could ever have imagined. It remained only for the invited press to give us their overwhelming vote of confidence to make our success complete.

Our director, let's call him Ray, was a lovely fella. He understood the process I was going through in arriving at my own version of Billy, and he was sympathetic to the cause. So much so, that when he approached the press in the days prior to the first night performance, he told them not to

146

worry themselves about criticism but rather to just enjoy themselves, as he was convinced, they would have a great time. He meant well. He did not want to put the cast under pressure to perform, but he had, at the same time, effectively stripped us of any evidence of our production's immense triumph, which went duly unreported.

He had not intended the press write nothing. It had just been his pleasant way of saying he would not put his cast under pressure to satisfy the papers. It was, if you like, similar to the woman who says, "Don't bother getting me anything for my birthday, I have got everything I need". We all know what she really means.

Nonetheless, he was as disappointed as the rest of us when he realised the implications of his aside. We searched in vain for a review to satisfy our hunger for approval and although contact was made with the papers it was too late. We would have only our own memories.

In the days leading up to the production run at the Arts Centre, and in the days following our achievements as an ensemble, Ray was inconsolable. We spent moments in celebration of the reception we had been given, of the many handshakes, the drinks we had been bought, the hugs and the words of admiration. We also discussed the future, acting and directing. And banking. And academies of dramatic art such as RADA. I was pumped up and I was feeling invincible. I was certain that with the right training I could give acting a go, and moreover make it a career. My director was equally convinced, and he then and there offered to help me apply for a suitable college in London. Friends and cast colleagues joked with me that I was going to end up on Coronation Street.

It is at times like these that decisions need to be made, important life defining decisions. Decisions that I have rarely found easy. Having said that, a decision not to take chances is always perhaps much easier to make than one to face up to challenges head on. I was sure that I was up to it, and had no doubt that if I was given the opportunity, I would take it firmly in my grasp, but it is important to realise what was being said there. I was not yet prepared to make the decision for myself. Had someone sorted it for me I would be there, signing on the dotted line. Domestic circumstances dictated that I continue to act responsibly, continue to bring home the bacon, continue with the day job. Did I have the guts to put myself and my ambitions first? Was I prepared to risk what I had at home? If I committed myself to the theatre with all the financial implications of years without a fixed income what would happen to my relationship?

As always, it was easier to do nothing than something. Don't rock the boat. Don't risk looking silly. I knew that, ultimately, I just could not raise the subject for discussion. I felt sure that I would be laughed at, mocked, teased and gently ridiculed. An actor? Don't be daft. Years of academy followed by an uncertain future.

My director had more faith in me than those immediately surrounding me. We talked about the risks and implications. Then, when the production ended, we saw less and less of each other, and gradually the dream faded and I returned to the daily grind of the banking world.

Now then, I could take you to a copy of my next play in the bookshelf at the top of the stairs in my house. It marked a sea-change in the level of my acting and in the quality of the material we were performing. It was a comedy again, but this time the characters were much better drawn, they had a depth to them that Tomb characters lacked. It also had a message of sorts, and more importantly it dealt with adult themes.

I wasn't desperate to get a part, but at auditions I found myself competing against several men of my age for what seemed like two suitable parts. One was Father Mullarkey, an Irish priest, the other Derek, a Teddy boy in his late teens. The play, an award-winner by Mary O'Malley was called 'Once A Catholic' and was a hilarious comedy about the resilience of children to survive in spite of, and not because of, the indoctrination of their upbringing, based on Mary O'Malley's own schooldays in the 1950s. There were to be 10 females in the cast and just 4 males, one of which would be a very old foreign music master, which just about ruled me out.

I lied: I was **desperate** to get a part, and I acted my socks off at the readthrough. I was Father Mullarkey, so I was. Then I was Derek, my Harlesden accent as 'arlesden as I could get it.

Both parts would be out of character for me. One, an Irish priest full of religious platitudes and sayings, the other a young lothario in the making, happy to get off with any of the several Mary's attending the local school.

149

I was not surprised to get the part of Derek, but I was over the moon. The part called for me to adopt a young man of the world attitude, carefree and randy, snogging girls left right and centre if they would allow him. This called for some serious acting!

It would also call for me to grow my hair into a duck's arse and grease it back, to wear blue suede creeper shoes and drape jacket with a Slim-Jim tie. Once your hair was greased into a D.A. it rarely looked right at the bank the following day, and you can imagine the looks I got at the enquiry desk.

We were blessed with a fantastic director, Shelley Sutton, who knew exactly what she wanted from us and how to achieve it. She was steadfast in her attention to detail and worked us hard. The result was a well drilled cast and a slick very funny production. It did not go entirely to plan however. In the play Derek tries it on with several of the girls, thankfully all called Mary. Rehearsal for the seduction scenes was going well, at first without actual contact, then with hands and lips. And in the case of Patti, who played one of the Marys, tongues too. Extraordinarily embarrassing for a married man. Throughout rehearsals Patti, who was engaged to be married, and expecting too, continued to thrust tongues where I had not expected tongues to be thrust, until I admit to enjoying and looking forward to it. The press came in and took our photos, which appeared two days prior to the show.

Then, when I turned up for the dress rehearsal, the director dropped the bombshell. Patti had had a miscarriage, and there was no chance she would be available for the show. One of the other girls would have to step in, script in hand. She had no qualms about having to read the part, but her boyfriend would be in the audience, and tongues were definitely out of the question. She was clearly worried about what her boyfriend would say, and told me so. What could I do about the situation if I had to stick rigidly to the script?

I hatched a plan. My plan was to make the kiss under the lamp-post as humorous as possible, and by exaggerating it, take the physicality of the situation out of it. At the final rehearsal I played it cool, going through the motions, pecking her on the cheek to reassure her. Come the first night however, I took her firmly in my arms, leaned over her, bent her backwards and planted a big kiss full on her lips, whilst at the same time buckling her at the knees, while she uttered muffled noises of surprise and flapped her arms around in a comic submission. It brought the house down, and her worries evaporated as we left stage right.

The play also marked the start of my musical theatre career. Derek reveals the singer in him while trying to charm Mary Mooney into performing certain sexual moves on him. The stage directions call upon Derek to imitate Elvis badly, but it went against my better nature to do a bad imitation! Don't forget all those early nan performances of Harry Worth and Freddie Davies. I cleverly skimmed over the song in rehearsals before giving it my all on the night, all shook up, and the whole audience rose to its feet, including my parents. Critics all agreed that the production had been a roaring success, and we celebrated with a cast and backstage party at the Wyvern Theatre. 'A peek behind convent walls' said Lynn Barlow in the local press, 'delighted a full house with its controversial humour', with 'notable backing from Malcolm Harris'.

Other productions followed. 'A Man for all Seasons' and 'Enter a Free Man' provided me with more opportunities to explore my talent for the stage.

Tom Stoppard's first play 'Enter a Free Man' was another comedy, and again I was given the lead role of Riley, a hapless inventor with a family falling out of love with him. The production failed to live up to its billing, and although there were some nice moments, the thrill and excitement I had experienced in Billy was no longer present. The director, to my mind, lacked the experience to make a success of the play. Some of the cast were struggling with lines and stage directions, some even struggled with pacing, leaving the story plodding along and losing much of the humour of the excellent writing. Effort was undoubted, but results continued to be inadequate. I was losing commitment myself, and the run ended with disappointing reviews. 'The company set itself a hard task.'

'There were some nice moments particularly between Malcolm Harris as hapless George, Sandra Warr, his daughter, and Richard Parker, as Harry the spiv. But in other places it dragged.' said the press.

When your ambitions begin to fade, it takes a big intervention to make a U-turn, and such an intrusion was 'A Man for all Seasons'. This was a huge production, by a different acting company, the Wyvern Community Drama Company. It was the first play that would allow me to tread the boards at the Wyvern Theatre and to go on tour with a production outside Swindon. I had auditioned more out of habit than ambition. Lots of juicy parts for male actors. I had been up against actors with Equity cards, a real and proper test of my credentials. I had been rewarded with a 'nice' part, not top billing this time, but Richard Rich, a significant player in the story of Sir Thomas More.

I was still working full time, and rehearsing every evening. We were rehearsing on stage at the Wyvern one night when my car was broken into, my work suit and my bank cards strewn over the car park, my car windows smashed, followed by a late-night appearance at the local nick to report the break-in.

We played the Wyvern and then did a few days at the Link, a local shopping centre theatre. By the time we moved on to the fabulous Wilde Theatre in Bracknell, travelling up and back daily after work, I was a shadow. The rush to get made up and dressed in historical costume, the weight and excessive warmth of three layers of wool, the 'gold' chain and feathered hat, the nervous wait to go on stage, all of this had started to take its toll. After the first act came to a close, I came off stage a wreck, gasping for breath and feeling faint. The doctor was called, pronouncing me fit but exhausted. A fellow actor went on for me, script in hand, and concerned audience members asked about my welfare.

And right there, backstage at the Wilde Theatre, Bracknell my acting career, such as it was, came to an abrupt end. I was suffering from nervous exhaustion, and before it could put my job at jeopardy, I just had to call it a day.

In fairness, I gave it one more go, by auditioning for the Wyvern's big production of 'My Fair Lady' singing 'On the Street where you live'. Once the pianist gave me a note, I proceeded to sing an octave higher than my natural voice would go, before making the decision that I was never going to make acting my career.

Banking was not the answer nor the antidote, though it took more heartache and illness before I was bright enough to realise that I needed to be creative if I was to be happy at all in life. I never returned to the stage and still wonder to this day where I would have been if I had been brave enough to make the move. Albert Square? Coronation Street? Between jobs do you think?

10. MY FAVORITE ACTORS

Gene Hackman

Tom Hanks

Meryl Streep

Keeley Hawes

Lacey Turner

Tom Conti

Keira Knightly

11. NO SHAKESPEARE, BUT ENJOYABLE NONETHELESS

This book finds me writing my third proper piece of prose. First of all, came a play, 'Being so Cheerful', then my first children's picture book, 'Shubby and the Mammacs: The Golden Crown' followed by 'A Mere Mortal'.

I toyed with writing as a child. My compositions had always been well received at school, but, as you know, they finished abruptly once the required length had been reached, and they all went home for tea. I always enjoyed using language. Hadn't I ended up studying French and German at university. I tried my hand at poetry at school too, but then doesn't everyone at some time or another?

By the time I left Swansea I had just about had enough of literature, certainly reading books, and for a long while I read very little except text books to pass my banking exams, which in themselves took 3 long years.

I realised quite early on, that if I ever put pen to paper, it was likely to fizzle out part way through. My track record was there, in my school reports. Promising, but somewhat curtailed, a bit like my grammar school story.

156

There was always the knowledge that I just couldn't draw that had prevented me from penning a kids' book. I stored up an idea I had about a little girl with magical friends for absolutely years while I searched for an illustrator I could work with. That search was always more in my head than expressed outwardly.

When she was little, our Rachael was extremely blonde to the point of being white-haired. She loved being taken to the gardens to feed the ducks either on Newquay boating lake or in Truro's Boscawen park. She also had invisible friends who, if you weren't careful, you could find yourself about to sit on when you hovered above a sitting room chair or settee. A germ of an idea formed even then – some 25 years earlier.

But if I was to write my story, or rather Rachael's story as Shubby, I really needed that artist to translate my words into pictures.

Then one Christmas, my wife Denise invited me to a pub buffet to celebrate a colleague's birthday, engagement or leaving, not sure what, maybe it was just Christmas itself. The pub was packed, and one by one Denise introduced me to some of her colleagues that I had not previously met. One of the ladies, Rebecca, listened to me rabbiting on about wanting to write a children's book, and mentioned that her husband Martin did a bit of illustrating. I almost literally bit off her hand. Did she think he would be interested in illustrating my book which was in its early stages? In truth it was still all in my head.

After a couple of faulty starts, where neither Martin nor myself took the other seriously, we met up in a coffee bar in the Winter Gardens on a frosty morning to discuss the project. We had never met before, so I suggested I wore a red carnation to identify myself, and our sense of humour seemed to click. Within minutes, Martin was scribbling pencil drawings of Shubby: before my eyes my dream was becoming reality. He had a special talent, that was evident. Now I needed to write, edit and crop my story so that Martin could read it for himself.

Martin seemed to like the concept. Even better, he could visualise the magical friends and make them real.

I got to work, writing on page after page of a tiny notebook, editing and refining as I went. I had so many ideas, too many in fact. I ended up with over 1500 words, far too many for a compact children's story.

We met up in our office at the Winter Gardens, this time Martin had some colour drawings to show me, while I was able to pass him the final draft.

Time passed. Martin had been going to start drawing the story page by page, starting with the cover. In the meantime, I had taken on the task of cutting huge chunks from the storyline. I really needed no more than 500 words. I brought in Rachael to test it out at school, and following a reading to her class she advised me on what was appropriate and what I should discard.

Still nothing from Martin, except for a front cover with the Mammacs spelled incorrectly with a K. I was disheartened and began to think that I was the only one who cared about the project. I should have known better! Martin had a full-time job just as I did, and his time was limited. Good as his promise though, he began to come up with picture after picture. Time for another meet.

Little café table, page after page of printed word, pictures of all the characters spread out, we worked together on the final image of the book, excluding this picture, editing the script to fit the drawing, until we had a rough storyboard for the book. Martin's pictures of the Mammacs were perfect, just as I had imagined them: cheeky monkey Munty, lanky young Gerry Giraffe, and never-give-up penguin Percy Vere. Together with my little Shubby with her curly blonde hair, we were ready to begin the search for a publisher. We considered it wise to find ourselves an agent.

You have a question I can tell. Where does the name Shubby come from? I wanted to relate the girl of my story to my own little girl, now in her mid-twenties, so I ruled out using her own name. As a child however, Rachy had, like most kids, her own language. Until she could formulate words as we knew them, she often chatted away to herself as she played with dolls, ponies and sometimes pebbles. Her conversation sounded a lot like 'shubbay, shubba, shubby, shusha, shubs' and we could not help but smile at her. It seemed only natural therefore to call my hero Shubby.

Clutching my 'Artists' and Writers' Yearbook' in one hand, I noted down all the agents who claimed to include children's books in their catalogue, and wrote them all a nice letter of introduction, attaching – mainly by email – the script, together with a couple or three of the illustrations, and, as is my wont, sat back and waited for the acceptances to flood in. Sure as eggs are eggs, in poured the replies, and as friendly was the wording, and as encouraging as the comments were, referring me time and again to the Artist and Writers Yearbook, the answer was the same: agents receive several thousand books a year and of those choose but two or three, sometimes none at all.

They say that it is important to keep going. They say that even the greatest of authors meet with rejection. They say that you must persist and never consider giving up. Whoever they are, they can't have felt as cheesed off as I did, or they would have just shrivelled up and conceded defeat.

I wasn't naïve. I knew the odds when we wrote the book. I just made the mistake of thinking that my story was special, and now no-one would get to see it in print.

It hadn't been my first attempt at writing.

For many years I had heard people joke, 'You're not putting me in a care home!' I had heard it on television, in family gatherings, in comedy sketches, and it had been one of those light-hearted statements said without real meaning. Recently however I had been involved in more than one long drawn out conversation where the subject of a residential care home had been real and pressing. As a society we were becoming more and more aware of the sneaky ailment that is dementia, the new posh word for senility we thought. Alzheimer's was another concept we were encountering without knowing too much about it. Friends talked openly about having to put family members in a home, family members who were not only forgetful but violent too, and impossible to live with.

I had first-hand knowledge of the subject in my close family as well, and determined to write about the topic by way of catharsis.

In my office canteen each lunchtime, people became aware that I was no longer doing the sudoku in the paper as I had been accustomed. I had in front of me reems of paper and was studiously scribbling away. Forty minutes at a time, I was writing a play. I decided to call it 'Being so Cheerful' after a phrase taken from an old wartime radio programme, 'It's that man again' known colloquially as ITMA. The character in question, Mona Lott, (say it out loud!), a depressed laundrywoman, would tell you all her woes before saying, 'It's being so cheerful as keeps me going'.

The play features an elderly couple, in poor health, trying to come to terms with old age, dementia and the prospect of a care home. It is obviously a comedy.

Never published, I have offered the play to local theatre groups and entered it in regional playwriting competitions, so far without success. I still have a great deal of faith in my script, especially in view of the importance of the subject matter, and feel that there is mileage in it, though I fear that it may take a real genius to appreciate it.

Shubby, meanwhile was without a publisher. Of course, I had heard about self-publishing. What I knew suggested that it would be expensive, difficult and not very satisfactory. I needed to explore the possibilities however if I was to see my little book in print. In the event, I came across Blurb and Bookwright, and after downloading their templates, spent not an inconsiderable time fitting my book to their specifications, with the result that I was able to print a sample, which thrilled me rigid! There right in front of me was my book, Shubby and the Mammacs, and a shiver ran up my spine.

Small adjustments were necessary to the margins, the colour and some text before I was happy with the final version, which I ordered in a small trial batch to sell to friends. I also arranged for the book to be sold through Amazon worldwide, and took it to local events and craft fairs, and signing sessions.I set Shubby up with her own Facebook page and she was delighted to receive 'likes' by the dozen from fans the world over. At the time of writing Shubby has yet to make that big breakthrough. Had I the inclination and the money to advertise I would take the project further. I fully intended Shubby to have a series of adventures, for there to be a shorter snappier simpler version for tinies, and for more of the Mammacs to make their entrance in similarly exciting adventures. Am I using finances as an excuse? I have the time after all.

Naturally I have tried to publicize Shubby. I booked myself into a bed and breakfast in Cheltenham, and as an ex-local I gate-crashed the Literature Festival in 2017. I took plenty of copies of my picture-book with me. There were the inevitable groups of schoolchildren visiting the festival, and I rather brazenly approached their accompanying teachers with free copies to read, with the proviso that if they liked it, they would leave a review on Facebook. What I failed to tell them in my haste, was that while Mal Harris did not have his own page, Shubby and the Mammacs did. No wonder this venture proved somewhat unsuccessful.

While I was in town, I arranged to meet up with Roger Apted for a drink. The idea was, that we would have a couple of pints before heading over the road to an evening of open mike, where like-minded authors could voice their concerns, recite poetry or give a brief talk. Still feeling miffed that celebrities were getting a fairer shake than us men in the street, I had written a lengthy poem mocking the ease with which the likes of Chris Hoy, David

Walliams and even Theo Walcott had been able to publish children's stories, while my little book languished publisher-less. I thought it was so very clever, and I was determined to recite it at the open mike night. After all, there might just be a publisher sat quietly at the back who would, just like in the movies, see my potential and snap me up.

The drinks session went well enough, and Roger and I reminisced about our school days. We kept an eye on our watches because Roger knew the plan, and in good time we crossed to the literature festival grounds. There were several tents, where authors including Hilary Clinton were due to speak, and one in particular was earmarked for the open mike gathering.

Entering the pavilion, Rog and I could not help but notice how quiet things were. The food stands were all closed and just one bar remained open. One or two people drifted in and then out again. Still it was only ten to.

I couldn't help but notice that the mikes usually in the corner were missing. Still, there were nine or so minutes to get everything ready.

Then around 100 women came into the marquee and strode up to the bar. That was more promising. An audience at least!

The atmosphere lifted and the sound of spirited young ladies filled the air. This was going to be a successful occasion I could sense.

Then, one by one, or in some cases two by two, the ladies exited the tent, until just Roger and I were left, stunned by the sudden evacuation. We were alone again, and the bar was closing too. Maybe, just maybe, the event had been cancelled? Give it ten minutes eh? Finish our pints and see what happens.

Nothing happened, except that we said our good-byes and set off for home, or the b and b in my case. I felt disappointed, let down by the festival organisation. The least they could have done was pin up a notice to let us know about the cancellation. After all it was organised in the name of the Times and they should have been reliable.

I returned to my digs, and I don't know why but I pulled out my festival guide, a 60-page booklet containing all the schedules and a map of the grounds. Maybe I was going to check out the following day's timetable, I don't know.

I wanted to just check the time of the open mike session, before I went to bed. Yes, it had been today at 10 pm.

In the grounds opposite Montpellier bars and restaurants.

In the main pavilion, right?

No, not in the main pavilion, where I, Roger and 100 women had been sat, but in the tent next to the entrance, some 50 yards away. I could hardly believe my eyes, but there it was, in black and white. I had been preoccupied with how to deliver my brutal attack on the famous and their agents so much so that I had taken my eye off the most important ball of all, the venue, and bang, my opportunity to make my statement had vanished in a moment of crass stupidity and ineptitude.

165

Not unnaturally, Roger asked the following day what had happened, and perhaps bravely, I admitted my error. We laughed, oh how we laughed.

I still have not broken even with Shubbs, and I feel guilty that I have given my illustrator Martin not a bean for all his brilliant drawings.

12. THE NEXT DAVID BAILEY?

The first photo I ever took was in Weston-super-Mare. I must have been about 8 years of age, perhaps even younger, and I would have borrowed dad's camera, with its monochrome film, which you wound on by hand. I remember being intrigued by the consecutive numbers that showed in the red see-through panel indicating how many shots you had taken. F11 for sunny days and f8 when it turned cloudy. I can't remember using f11 that often.

I still have the prints. I must have taken around 8 pictures, mostly of the beach, of the pier, of donkeys and carts on the sand. Surprisingly, the subjects of the photos are central. Cameras then had no focusing mechanism. You set the f stop, pointed and clicked.

From seeing the results of my efforts, I fell in love with photography. To see those 2.5 by 1.5 inch black and white pictures now and to think that I still have them shows the extent to which they made an impression on me at that young age.

Dad gave me his old camera. I used it on holidays with the family for years.

And then one day I decided to buy a camera of my own. I purchased a second-hand Zenit, a Russian beginner's camera with a cracking lens. The Zenit was my introduction to the single lens reflex. I continued to mess about with single use cameras, and those plastic cameras with the exploding flash bulbs as did most kids of my age, but I really wanted to create pictures with a bit of style, using the available light. In addition to portraits of people I knew, I started shooting abstracts of recurring themes, lines of lamp-posts, rows of houses, strings of geese, anything with a distinct pattern.

Photography remained a major hobby, but my equipment failed to keep pace with technology and my pictures were OK but no better.

I read just about every magazine there was on the market. I spent hours looking at all the best photos. I learned as much as I could about the technical aspects of my hobby without ever putting many of them into practice. I knew all about f-stops, apertures and depth of field, telephoto lenses, film and slides, flash-lit photos, but still didn't have the camera I required.

Then I got the competition bug, and discovered the indoor studio. At more or less the same time as my burgeoning interest, my day job was becoming increasingly stressful. I spent much of my spare time taking pictures specifically for magazine competitions, some of which involved asking friends to pose for me in the studio. I attended photographic shows and continued to learn. I hired models and went through the nervous process of getting to know them quickly and to put them at ease, while trying not to show them that I was just as anxious as they were.

I had so many ideas in my head, and now it was approaching a time when I would make one of the biggest decisions in my photographic life. I had seen how the studio set-up worked, talked to the studio owner about his involvement and his potential income, and I was duly intrigued.

My latest camera was a new Pentax, the M series, an MG, followed by the SFX, which introduced automation in a big way. It also allowed for the indoor lights to be connected direct to the flash hot-shoe which would be essential if I was going to do more studio work.

Stresses and resulting illness put paid to the banking world, but not before time. Banking had run its course.

I was now out of work.

It was just like a lightning bolt. I knew immediately what I wanted to do. I wanted my own studio. Dave at my local photographic shop was 'the man'. He had contacts all over, and he treated my ambitions seriously, after all I was about to spend a fair wedge of money! He was so helpful though, and through him and his team I purchased lights, umbrellas, backing papers, stands, tripods and baffles.

House sold, and settled in Truro, I launched my search for a studio. It had to be sizeable, accessible and have its own facilities. There had to be one major room for the photography, and at least one other room for an office, and if possible, an additional space for a changing room. I would need to consider the needs and comfort of any models I engaged.

I had taken note of the way the Swindon studio had been set up, with its index of models, and I determined to replicate the arrangement, but to include a portrait and commercial wing to the business.

Dad came with me to suss out the potential studios. One was far too small, in one the ceilings were too low, another was on the third floor making access too difficult.

Then, we visited a second floor flat with 4 rooms including a small kitchen. One of the rooms was the perfect studio size, and just down the corridor there was a toilet. With a lick of paint, I felt sure it would be a great prospect. It had its own locked door, brilliant, and stairs to the floor were wide and welcoming. On the door was a sign – The Dyslexic Society. We joked that it should have said The Dyxlesic Society – not terribly politically correct, but then we weren't back then.

On the ground floor was a large and well-established music shop selling pianos, guitars, instruments and sheet music, and it had its own entrance on the street. A Chinese restaurant lived above the music shop, and access was via the same stairway as the flat. Provided I could have my own keys to the main doors, I would not be restricted to restaurant opening hours, and the shop would provide a steady stream of passing custom. A lift would have been welcome, but I was running out of time and patience, not to mention rooms to investigate. I was convinced by the layout to make an offer for the flat, and within days I had signed up. I now was the owner of a photographic studio. Mallyn Studio was up and running.

I soon learned my first lesson, and it was not a nice one. Remember the jealousy and rivalry I encountered in the radio station? It was as nothing when compared with that in the world of photos, and I learned all about it the hard way.

Before I could advertise my studio and all that it offered, I had to decide on a strategy. I decided to write a newspaper article notifying the world of my opening date, and sent my press release off. I also decided to place adverts weekly for a four-week period to kick things off. I considered that once I had my first satisfied customers, word of mouth would prove my best advertising strategy.

Nervously, I had wandered around Truro searching for my models. The search had started ever so timidly, clutching my calling cards in one hand, my encouraging words memorised, my smile fixed on my face, eyes peeled for attractive girls. It sounds idyllic, but it was scary.

The first girl I approached worked in a department store. I showed her my card and smiled. That in itself was not going to do it. I offered a trial shoot and cash per session. She looked vaguely interested, and at least she didn't say 'No'. She asked me how old I thought she was. I should have known better, but I was having a conversation and got drawn in! Maybe late 20s I ventured, possibly 28? A young looking 28 at that.

I think I know what you are wondering. I was wrong, but by how much, and had it done my quest any permanent harm? As it happened, I had been just the ten years out, but which way? Not so bad if she had hit the late thirties, but sadly, Liz was 18 and not 38.

I thought I had blown it, but fortunately for me she took it well and laughed it off, melting the ice in the process. Liz was my first recruit.

I found my next model in Blockbusters, a video shop – remember them? - then another at Marks and Spencer, one at the local pub, two in a women's clothes shop. I built up a nice portfolio, stopping sixth-formers in the street, a local jeweller's sales girl, coffee shop waitresses and a classic-shoe shop sales lady.

All of the young ladies came to the studio for a try-out, with the promise that I would give them copies of the best photos. Some of the girls were happy to pose in swimwear or mini-skirts, one or two went even further and happily stripped topless, with the incentive of being invited to evening group glamour sessions. These sessions meant significant reward and the chance of getting started in the modelling world, with the proviso that I would be present at all times to ensure things did not get out of hand. I loved each and every one of my girls, and I did my best to involve as many of them as I could in the sessions without favouring any one of them. It had to be a two-way street though. Once a girl had let me down by failing to turn up, or by being late without letting me know she had been delayed, her name would be removed from the rota.

Many of the models were either married or in relationships, some shy, some less so, and I was utterly determined to be thoroughly professional in my day to day dealings with them. There were always snide comments and suggestive nudges whenever the subject of my occupation came up, but I was thankful that goodwill existed on both sides and I can honestly say that there was never the slightest hint of a transgression. And this, in spite of the obvious temptation that I placed before them.

I did my best too. to make any of my own photographic sessions with them as much fun as possible. These sessions tended to be portfolio builders.

One pretty young blonde girl, Anna, was the model I selected to illustrate an article I was writing for Pentax magazine. The article was about how, as a beginner studio-photographer, you should approach your first assignment with a model, and it explained how best to make him or her feel relaxed, and thus get the best results. We shot photos of Anna, with a towel wrapped around her torso on top of her clothes, leaving her shoulders bare. Shots of her top half, subsequently cropped, would allow the impression of her being shot topless, but without the intrinsic embarrassment often encountered by beginners.

In the same session we shot motion shots of Anna jumping into the air to illustrate how it might be possible to break the ice and to put your model at ease. The article for Pentax required specimen pictures to accompany the script, and it was during this session that I uttered the immortal words, 'Can you open your legs just a little more for me, Yes, that's it, lovely!'

173

I then added that it was a good job there was nobody stood outside the door listening in! The two of us just fell about laughing, and that was, in itself, a fine illustration of how we often reduced any tension between the photographer and his subject.

To kick off my professional work I engaged the services of some enthusiastic teenagers to act out a story for one of those Dundee-based picture magazines, taking them to a local fast-food outlet for photos based on a storyboard I had drawn up. Tanya and a 'boyfriend' adopted poses and pulled faces to enact a typical girl-meets-boy tale of love and lost love, to which bubbles of dialogue would be added later at the publishers.

"I have a fond memory of doing a photo story shoot for a magazine in the burger restaurant near to the studio. You were so supportive and professional that it all went to plan and you got the pics you needed. I think I had to pretend to slap my current boyfriend and go off with someone else" Tanya recalls. "I just remember how professional and organised you were. I was very much in awe of your ability and creativity."

Have we drifted off subject again?

Oh yes, I was telling you about the lesson I learned, wasn't I?

Somehow and somewhere, I don't remember where or when, I met another photographer, let's call him Trevor, because I have a feeling that was his name. He seemed a lovely guy and we got to talking about my ambitions for my studio. He did a lot of weddings, an area of photography I was not all that keen on getting too involved in to be honest. Thinking about it, our meeting could have been at a wedding fair, because he had with him two young ladies, who he introduced to me as his assistants. I had been contemplating running an advert with pictures of the studio facilities, the lights, background, brollies and so on, and Trevor kindly offered to send his assistants over to demonstrate the equipment, dressed beautifully and pointing in the iconic way that 'The Price is Right' girls and boys would have done.

A time was arranged. I turned up at the appointed hour, and true to his word Trevor dropped the two girls off at my studio. They seemed impressed as we sipped coffee and chatted over the shoot I envisaged. Yep, they were more than happy with the plan, and slipped into the backroom to change into fetching swimsuits. They were attractive young ladies, one blonde and curvy, the other slim and pretty. The session was perfect in every way, and we achieved some excellent results, though of course in them there days we would have to wait for the prints to come in the post.

We parted, with the promise of some potential work for them, if all could be arranged with Trevor. The pictures arrived, and I set to editing and placing my advertisements. Then I got a phone call. From Trev. Good old Trev.

How had the session gone? Was I happy with the results? Weren't they lovely girls? How much was I willing to pay for the copyright on the photos?

Can you hear the pennies drop? Ping, ping, ping, until almost a pound's worth had fallen before I realised what a mug I had been taken for. You idiot

Harris. What did you think – that this was a generous, unselfish gesture on the part of a potential rival? Moreover, I would have to publicise HIS girls in my advert and pay for the privilege!

I did know all about copyright, hadn't I spent enough time reading about it. Business practice though? I was I guess naïve in the ways of the world, and I couldn't understand how anyone could take advantage of someone else in the way that our Trev had done. Lesson learned, move on.

So now, I had just about everything in place. I had a stable of nice young models, all pleasant and charming, all ready to pose for tasteful pictures, I had the right set-up for portraits, and I was ready to advertise my skills to the commercial world of Cornwall.

In the meantime, I was invited to a wedding up country, and as usual I took my trusty camera with me. It was just as well I did. Michelle was a friend of my then partner, a work colleague in fact.

The weather was disappointing. Brollies were out, and on arrival at the church I thought the bride and her father under the trees as they approached the church would make for a nice picture. I continued to snap away, and their huge brolly added to the atmosphere of the damp leaves scattered all around. What light there was reflected off the wet path.

After the ceremony there was a hiatus. The rain continued to fall steadily. And the photographer had failed to turn up.

Michelle knew of my business plans, and she was desperate for a lasting record of her wedding. The reception was due to take place at the local sports centre, and we adjourned there for the buffet without a photo being taken. You are no doubt two sentences ahead of me, and you would be absolutely correct. Against the background of the netball court walls I took some smashing pictures of the wedding party, complete with the colourful court markings on the shiny wooden floor. I sold a significant number of copies, though admittedly at vastly reduced prices because of the circumstances, but the best images made an impressive poster display for my studio, and served to convince me that weddings could provide a decent contribution to my overall income.

For the first couple of months I spent a lot of time in the studio by the phone. I couldn't afford an answerphone. Occasionally it would ring and there would be a conversation about where I was, how much this or that portrait would cost, and the phone went down again without any appointment having been made. Day by day, however, as people saw the newspaper adverts, the photos in the street doorway, the flyers I had distributed locally in shops and businesses, appointments crept up in number. The music shop's resident Alsatian dog posed for his portrait, while the Chinese restaurant engaged me to snap the interior of the restaurant for a name-checked display behind glass outside the building.

Tanya posed for photos at the first of our regular theme nights. Her role was as a tennis player, and we set the studio up to resemble a tennis court, complete with all kinds of props, rackets, ball tubes, players' and umpire's chair. I think I loaned her a contemporary tennis shirt if I remember correctly. She looked great in her headband, and we attracted at least 5 fee-paying and keen photographers who all became regulars.

As Tanya recalls, "I was very much in awe of your ability and creativity. As it was the first time I had ever been in a studio or had pictures taken I was understandably nervous. You always explained things fully and put me at ease. I would say you had massive potential as a photographer and you obviously had a keen eye for a fantastic picture."

Future themes included a barn scene complete with straw bales, girls at their make-up, and lingerie in a bedroom setting. The tills started to ring.

Outside the studio, I got one job via the company that placed my advert, and it turned out to be a strange one too. While I was on the phone to them, they asked if I would be available to take a staff picture for their own press release. They were a fairly new company, and they wanted to advertise their presence in the expanding market.

I attended their workplace, and lined the staff up in the car-park for the usual left-to-right press photo which I took from an upstairs window. On a dull day, I wasn't all that impressed with the available light, but the session went well enough. They had won an award too, and wondered while I was there, whether I would take some more images of a presentation of the award indoors. I was happy to oblige.

Inside, there were drinks and sandwiches, and on the opposite side of the room, a trophy, and a lady who seemed somewhat familiar. The boss took up his position alongside the award, and the lady, dressed smartly in black, picked it up and smiled as she handed it over. Of course, *that* was who it was, for television viewers of Hi-de-Hi, and lovers of xylophones everywhere, Ruth Madoc, much more glamorous than I could remember seeing her before.

In fact, considering how short my career in photography ultimately turned out to be, it was remarkable that Ruth Madoc was not the only celebrity I snapped.

I took some lovely studio pictures of a local Truro woman and her two daughters, both together and individually. Indeed, one of the daughter's pictures found its way into my portfolio. It truly was a corker.

I promised to hand-deliver the results, as they only lived a street or two away, in fact they ran a business, a health food shop. They were, coincidentally, having a refit, and conversation turned to the re-opening of the shop in a few days' time. What would be nice, mum thought, would be if I could come along and take some marketing images of the new layout, and of the special guest that was coming along to re-open the shop, and subsequently, of the customers on the day.

I must be honest; I didn't quite catch the name of the bodybuilder that was due to open the shop. Had it been a man, I wasn't quite sure?

Well, unless men had long blond hair and painted finger-nails, this bodybuilder was definitely a female. In spite of her bulging thigh muscles and her deep voice she was clearly very feminine. Stripping off her sweater top she posed in the shop doorway, and inevitably we got talking. She had always kept fit, having been a bit of a runner when she was younger. Her face began to look familiar. What event had she been involved in? 400 metres. Hadn't she been married to another athlete? Yes, Bill Hartley. Of course, Donna Hartley! I had known her from the tele as Murray, and in a strange twist of fate, she had recently married one Bobby Knutt under his real name Wass, who I would meet up with and interview many years later in another of my many guises. Donna had been an Olympic medallist, and had won bodybuilding competitions, and after a hugely happy marriage to Bobby, died somewhat mysteriously, it was said, whilst sunbathing in her garden aged only 58. Bobby said of Donna that he wished he'd married his third wife (Donna) first.

Many of my customers were surprised by the size of the studio. One assignment by a local worm-farm dictated that I fill the room with straw bales. Families of four or five in number were almost lost in the vastness of the studio. Remember, I had room enough to replicate a barn, or centre court at Wimbledon, in my evening sessions for my regular group of glamour snappers, which were turning out to be one of the most popular items on offer.

I took bookings for the odd wedding, I mean I took bookings for occasional weddings, not peculiar weddings.

Bookings were still thin, however, when I went to London to meet up with an old friend from uni. He had obtained tickets to an evening buffet with a famous model, and invited me to come along. Remember that in the late 1980s The Sun's page three was highly popular, and models such as Sam Fox were instantly recognisable, one or two of them moving seamlessly into the pop world. Another well-known and much-loved model was the subject of the event in a plush discotheque. I was about to meet and greet the lovely Linda Lusardi, many men's page 3 favourite.

I must say that I found Linda delightful, well-spoken, bright and unassuming. She chatted with her fans in a relaxed manner, smiling at inane comments and sipping at her cocktail. At one point, I found myself alone with Ms Lusardi and able to raise the subject of my studio, in which she took great interest, feigned or not I was uncertain. It occurred to me, that what was required to provide a boost to the studio was the appearance of a 'name', and that furthermore I was currently sat alongside one of the biggest names in the photographic world.

Bull by the horns time. Linda was intrigued by the possibility of 'opening' the studio officially, and referred me to her management to see if a deal could be cut. The diaries suggested that the team would be in Cornwall in February of the following year, and that it was feasible that LL could be driven to Truro for a couple of hours to visit my studio.

There was no mention of cost. I imagined that if a visit was simply a sideshow to an already arranged event in the area that the charge would be minimal.

Days went by before I received a letter setting out a timetable for the day in question, to be a Saturday, together with a written down fee of several hundreds of pounds. I accept now that I made a huge mistake. First of all, I failed to either negotiate a lower fee, or to reject the offer completely and save myself money, which I could have spent on more reasonable advertising.

In the event, I went along with the management deal, and dreamt up a scheme to recoup some of my financial obligation. I decided to charge people to attend the opening, but to offer them a free photo with Linda, and to make appointments – like at the doctors' surgery – so that each paying guest would have fully ten minutes to chat with the lovely Linda. In retrospect, this was completely the wrong approach.

Linda's car was late. And it poured with rain. I had arranged a good dozen appointments prior to the day, so was guaranteed an income of sorts. If the weather had been kind, I was sure many more would take the opportunity to visit the studio. But the rain was incessant.

I laid on a small buffet in my office. As I set out the crockery and cutlery, I watched raindrops racing one another down the windows, while beyond the panes hardly a soul ventured out. No passing trade today, that's for sure.

I began to be concerned. that she would not arrive in time for the first appointment, in retrospect another reason why I had adopted the wrong tactics. I waited in the lean-to alongside the music shop, watching the hail, until suddenly, out of the mist, a car appeared, pulling up in the puddles outside the studio block. Out stepped Linda, and I moved in to welcome her, brolly at the ready, and to show her up to the studio as quickly as possible.

Before we really got going, the press arrived, together with a Newquay businessman who was to be featured in a photo release to celebrate the launching of a tennis court 'bubble' in Newquay itself. I wasn't sure that I had appreciated that my studio opening in Truro was to be used to reflect the success of others. No separate photos were taken of the opening ceremony, and I was duly side-lined in the picture that went to press as some kind of afterthought. Before I could raise any objections, the press were off.

I have to say, that the event itself was successful, but only to a point.

On a personal level, I found the page 3 model herself as charming as I had remembered. I heard her say to her tour manager between guests, 'I am so bored' and yet she was pleasant to everyone she met, posing endlessly for pictures, smiling and chatting, and even pouring tea for us when we took a break. It made me chuckle that Linda Lusardi was in my office eating cake. She was happy to muck in and cut me a piece of celebratory cake, and to raise a glass to the future of the business.

She kissed me as she took her leave, and wished me luck.

Was the occasion entirely how I foresaw it?

No, not exactly.

Would I have done it again?

Certainly, but so differently, with open access, a fanfare, flags and buntings, loads of photos and poster size prints on sale. I learned so many lessons, on so many different levels, but it was unquestionably an expensive way of alerting the public to the existence of my studio.

You might not believe it, but strangely, that was not my only connection with Page 3. Remarkably, page 3 made three appearances in studio life, each one reflecting the alternative views held by society of the day on the suitability of topless models in a national paper.

Many people, and it has to be said, mainly men, enjoyed their daily ogle. A bit of harmless fun, they would say. And it has to be admitted, many young ladies enjoyed not a little fame, success and financial gain from the profession. Glamour modelling was a lucrative career for some.

One morning there was a knock on the door, and in walked two women, one, a white woman possibly my age or slightly older, the other a black girl of no more than school age. Mum asked if I did portraits, and I imagined that they might want a family photo in my nice wicker settee.

Imagine my surprise when mum said that her daughter, still 15, wanted to be a glamour model, and wondered whether I could take some tasteful pictures of her to send to the Sun for her test. I had no problem with the concept, after all, the young lady clearly had her mother's blessing, but I knew my laws, and until she reached 16 there was no way she could pose topless. The daughter was pretty, shapely and bright – I immediately recognised the school she attended as one of Truro's top educational establishments. I found it refreshing that mum had not dismissed out of hand the prospect of her daughter modelling, and that she intended to keep a parental watch over the process rather than allow her to 'do her own thing'. I do know that both were delighted with the photos I took that day, and that they were promptly submitted to the Sun. I regret that I do not know how the audition went.

On the other hand, I took some lovely pictures of two young ladies together, good friends and very attractive with it. As perfect as they looked together, one of the girls had a super figure. She was intelligent too. She was fully aware of the kind of money that modelling could bring in. We discussed it briefly and she smiled almost knowingly.

The prints came back from the processors and they were just as positive as I had hoped. While the girls were in to collect their snaps, I gently raised the topic of modelling once more, after all, it was a money-spinner if you were prepared to give it a go, and once again she smiled, as if this was a huge compliment. At the same time, I recognised that she was too young to become involved in my group sessions.

Two days later the door to the studio burst open, and a young man hurtled into my office. His appearance suggested that he might be in the mood to rearrange my face, and it was with great difficulty that I eventually calmed him sufficiently to sit down and talk to me while I quietly trembled beneath my sweatshirt.

It seems as if he was the boyfriend of a girl who had recently had her photo taken at the studio, and the photographer had the temerity, not quite his words, to recommend a career as a page 3 girl. At the time, it did not occur to me to wonder why she had felt it necessary to mention this to her boyfriend, but one can only presume that she still felt some pride at the idea, and that she hoped he would see the potential, even if purely the financial repercussions. There was little point in my adopting that particular approach with said lad, who was still quietly incensed.

We never came to blows, but we came very close. I wondered whether he took a daily newspaper, and which one, however, this was not a path I followed, for obvious reasons.

One cold winter's day a skinny young thing walked into my office armed with a portfolio. I made her a cup of tea and we proceeded to chat about her modelling career. She brought out a topless photo of herself, said she had adopted a nom de plume, and very thoughtfully signed a copy of the picture for me to keep on file.

'Christiane' had been in the big smoke she said for several years, though just how old that would have made her when she started out, I wasn't prepared to guess, especially with my track record. She told me, with not an ounce of shame, that she had been seeing a famous married athlete, and was now looking for some work back in Cornwall.

I suggested a trial session and off she went to get changed.

Minutes later she emerged in a dressing gown and we started the session. After a few over-the-shoulder portraits, she slid the dressing gown off and tantalisingly posed nude. First of all, I am human. Second of all, I am a man. Third of all, what she was now offering was not on the agenda, and although this may surprise you, I asked her to get dressed and to leave. She foolishly imagined that what she was now offering, and it wasn't the opportunity to take her photo, would persuade me to give her regular employment. I wasn't that stupid, nor that desperate for that matter. I did see her again in local hostelries, but either she blanked me, or had completely forgotten the experience. I neither knew nor cared.

I was engaged to take photos of the Cornish Car Show at Truro City Hall, and then, at the same venue, a rather less showy set of Santa Claus in December 1987. I looked forward to snapping Santa with many of his little fans as they posed on his lap in the traditional fashion. It was the Saturday before Christmas. The Liberal Democratic Party was holding the event and local M.P. Matthew Taylor was due to attend. The day marked the anniversary of the tragic death in a car accident of previous M.P. David Penhaligon. So, the day's excitement was tempered somewhat by the presence of his widow Annette.

If my memory serves me well, I took something like 40 photos, recording names and address to send the pictures out in the post. Helping me with the names of the children and their parents was the very same Annette Penhaligon. Annette was very down to earth, and a lovely lady with no airs and graces, who became a firm friend, and someone I seemed to come into contact with on a fairly regular basis.

Mrs Penhaligon was a Carrick district councillor, whose photo, by a strange coincidence, I later took with all her colleagues for display on council notice-boards, while I myself was employed by the local council in its Housing Department. The managers there knew of my photographic background and asked me to take the head and shoulders snaps for a small fee, and it got me the afternoon off too, to fit in with the councillors' busy schedules. I guess it was inevitable that our paths would cross on the staircase from time to time.

By an even bigger coincidence, unbeknown to me, she was also a founding director of Pirate FM, and occasionally we would be surprised to find ourselves in the same company at radio station get-togethers. Our friendship survived the years until I left the county, a little while after the Queen conferred upon her a well-deserved Dame Commander of the British Empire. She married Robert Egerton in 1994, and I sincerely hope she is enjoying a happy retirement.

In spite of all my efforts to get jobs wherever I could, in the first year I made a whopping loss, but much of my capital expenditure was depreciated by my accountant, and in the second-year things were definitely improving. Bookings were up, the weekly model sessions were picking up and more people knew where to locate us. I attended 3 weddings too.

The music shop had moved out however, and the Chinese was now the only other occupant of our block. My domestic circumstances had changed suddenly and dramatically, and now the only household income to keep me and the cat from the scrapheap was my earnings from the business. It was a choice of carrying on the business or eating, and I knew on which side my bread was buttered, so to speak. Dad, to his credit, stepped in and offered me a loan to keep the business going, but my heart was temporarily no longer in photography, and, in time, I sold the equipment, keeping only the one camera, redecorated the office with white emulsion, and vacated.

Since the days of the studio I have maintained my interest in photography, switching inevitably to digital single lens reflex cameras and exchanging the old print slr for new or used lenses. I now use, exclusively, Canon cameras, and have been roped in to take official wedding pictures for my niece Becky and unofficial ones for her sister Louise, and occasional birthday and Christmas bashes for friends.

I like to gather my better photos of the year together in a calendar for family and friends, but as much as the lure to turn pro again raises its head from time to time, I have avoided the temptation to hurtle into the profession full-time once more, preferring to enjoy photography as a relaxing hobby.

I admit to entering competitions, including the Countryfile calendar competition. It never ceases to amaze me how pure amateurs achieve some of the results they do, especially the sight of nocturnal animals trotting along tree-lined roads by day, or groups of rarely seen mammals smiling simultaneously at the camera. Must just be luck, I suppose.

Nothing beats taking your camera out to a beach to snap breeding seals, or to the countryside to photograph castles or stately homes, to the seaside for boats and fishermen, or to the wildlife park to record encounters with tigers or polar bears. As we have got older though, it has become obvious to me that not everyone shares the thrill of standing in a cold field searching for skylarks, or on a clifftop hunting puffins, and I have to consider whether it is right to make family suffer while I wait for the sun to come up over a corn field, or attractive sheep or long-horned cattle to emerge from early morning mists.

Acting at university in the French Society, mainly Moliere.

And then in Swindon at the delightful Devizes Road Arts Centre. Tickets for the One Act Play Festival attractively priced at £1 or 50p!

SWINDON & DISTRICT THEATRE GUILD
ONE - ACT PLAY FESTIVAL
ARTS CENTRE   DEVIZES ROAD   SWINDON
Friday   2nd March   1984
COMMENCE 7.15 P.M.
No admission during course of each play

Row D.   Seat 6.
Price £1.00   Concession 50 p.

191

Above, with my 3 girl-friends in Billy Liar, and complete with 'perm' in my jim-jams. Left, as Richard Rich, touring 'A Man for all Seasons' Below, perhaps not my finest moment as hapless George Riley.

13. I ALMOST WENT OUT WITH MRS EAMONN HOLMES

I always liked Ruth. She brightened up local television, which was notoriously dull.

As a young boy I could fall in love with any television or film star at the drop of a hat. My friend David, aged 12, was in love with a girl, and for months I waited for an introduction, only to later discover that she was a celebrated television singer that David had admired from afar. It happened when you were young. I had a crush on Debbie Reynolds long before I even knew what a crush was.

But Ruth was real, more my age, we were both Pisceans, and she lived locally. How did our paths ever cross?

As a youngster I enjoyed being associated in any way possible with the famous. Being Trevor Hockey's cousin had been my way of becoming popular at university after all, getting tickets to Wales matches when he played, meeting players at the ground and occasionally at the station – they travelled by train in those days – or at their hotel. I revelled in being introduced to heroes such as Peter Rodrigues, the moustachioed Sheffield Wednesday lad playing full-back for Wales, as 'my cousin Malc'.

An autograph somehow brought me closer to the signatory's fame, and as the saying goes, I could bask in their glory.

One of my mother's cousins played for the Wales rugby side too, and we visited him at his home in Ebbw Vale more than once – big centre Arthur Lewis, who toured with the 1971 British Lions. I never thought to ask him for an autograph as we sat drinking tea and munching cakes.

At one time in the 1980s I actively collected autographs. I have long since sold most of the valuable ones, including that of the first man on the moon Neil Armstrong, which fetched a fair penny or two. I had found the name 'ACS' in a movie magazine I read. ACS, or Actors, Celebrities and Stars, promised that, for a small fee, they would provide you with a star's home or office address. If I really admired an actor or sportsman, I would send them a card asking for them to sign it and to send it back using the prepaid postage I enclosed with the request. Some kindly ignored the card and substituted pictures of their own, some quite extravagant like the photo of uptown girl Christie Brinkley draped in nothing but a strategically placed silk-like scarf, others more formal studio shots of head and shoulders. Britt Ekland signed hers in bright lipstick.

My most treasured responses were from Jack Nicklaus, the world's top golfer, Dudley Moore, surely one of the funniest and most talented comedians of all time, Brigitte Bardot, actress turned animal-rights activist, and my favourite singer Olivia Newton-John. I was also thrilled to receive the aforementioned signature from the first man on the moon, Neil Armstrong, from his home address.

I also wrote to theatres and sporting venues, receiving replies from Sir Lawrence Olivier, Sir John Gielgud, Tom Conti, Wonder Woman Lynda Carter, and tennis stars Steffi Graf and Martina Hingis, among many others. I guess I must have had well over 200 autographs.

My short note to each told in truthful terms of my admiration for their capabilities, whatever they might happen to be. There was never any risk of my asking an autograph of people I did not either revere or respect.

I have never come to terms with Instagram or Twitter. I tend to be at least 20 years behind technology. You know, waiting until it's safe or proven. The only two people I have ever followed on Twitter were Olivia, and Kelly Sotherton, the Olympic heptathlete. I wanted to congratulate her on her retirement, and later, on her belated medal from the Games, awarded as a result of cheats being disqualified upon review many years down the line, and so well-deserved. I did get Kelly's autograph too, but oddly, not on the occasion we met.

There's more to the story in reality.

I decided to go along to an athletics meet at Don Valley in Sheffield. It was a Sunday, and I had booked my ticket to see stars of track and field, including Dame Kelly Holmes in her final track race, and Justin Gatlin, American 100 metre champion. I took with me my trusty Canon point and shoot to capture the excitement. It took videos too, so I was thrilled with my seat, just two rows from the front, at the end of the long jump pit, and level with the finishing line. Perfect.

I hadn't planned to take so many pictures of the early races. The long jump turned out to be a ding-dong between an American and our own Chris Tomlinson. And I videoed an enthralling 400 metre junior race in which a young Martyn Rooney was running, so by the time Kelly Holmes made her spectacular arrival by helicopter my batteries were running down.

Not to worry, I couldn't foresee any need to take many more pictures.

It was then that my heart sank, as Kelly Holmes introduced the guest runners entered in her final track race. In amongst them was my heroine, and current sports crush, Kelly Sotherton. I watched the run unfold, warming my batteries in my hands to renew their charge, a trick I had used to great effect on many occasions, but to no avail on this occasion.

No photo of Kelly S. then, but I was sure that I could use my location to my advantage to get an autograph, as youngsters thronged around the retiring Dame Kelly, who was now within touching distance.

Out of the runners emerged Ms Sotherton, and she was coming straight towards me. I had my programme clutched in my left hand, my defunct camera tucked under my arm. All I needed was a pen. But the delightful Kelly was here, smiling at me, and I had no pen. I reached out my right arm, extended my open hand towards her. In what seemed like slow motion Kelly Sotherton took my hand in hers and gently squeezed it. Shaking hands had never felt like this before. She looked ever so slightly surprised, as if she was so used to signing bits of paper thrust in her direction, but had probably never been shaken by the hand. I was reluctant to let go, but I did succeed in continuing to breath, and Kelly moved on down the line, before skipping off to be interviewed for the BBC by Sally Gunnell.

On my way out of the complex, a young lady rushed towards me. She glanced down at her watch. "Oh shit" she exclaimed, and as she did so, I recognised this attractive woman as broadcaster Hazel Irvine, off the tele. I had seen her in Sheffield city centre, as she presented the World Snooker, but now she appeared shorter than I had imagined. She looked up at me, and said she was late for her train. Sorry, she apologised, she didn't use that kind of language. I said that I was certain she was telling the truth, and jokingly added that I wouldn't tell anyone, but I failed totally to tell her I was about to drive into town myself and could have got her to the station in no time at all. Talk about missed opportunities that day!

Do you know, I hate it when anyone says they have got a funny story, because I almost feel obliged to laugh or at least smile with a knowing look and a nod of recognition.

So, having said that, I have a funny story about a phone call I received one lunchtime at work.

It concerns a person I did obtain an autograph from, but puzzlingly, couldn't take home with me. The 'he' in question was a footballer from Scotland. His signature was written on a new customer card, while I dealt with his bank account transfer, and that signature card ended up with the bank's control clerk, probably Yvonne or Jayne, to open the account. I never thought to ask him for one for my collection.

I had approached the enquiries desk when the bell rang, and, there before me was a young man dressed fairly casually, but looking as if he might have been a sportsman of some sort, or at least a keep-fit fanatic.

I asked his name and occupation, and he said he was Tom McAlister, and he played professional football for Swindon, but was currently on loan with Bristol Rovers. I completed the paperwork to set his account up.

Strangely, I knew of Tom from his 63 appearances for Sheffield United around the time that my cousin Trevor had been at the club. I think it impressed him that his bank official knew of his reputation in the game. I also knew that he had sustained a bad injury which had curtailed his top-class career.

In the following few weeks Tom called into the bank to discuss progress with the transfer and I got to know him quite well, by sight at any rate. He was a brilliant goalkeeper, probably the best keeper never to play for Scotland. In just a short while, Tom was signed as number two to the charismatic Phil Parkes at West Ham United. They happened to be my favourite team at the time, and we chatted regularly when he called in for cash. Tom played well over 80 times for the Hammers.

Is it time for the funny bit yet?

Have patience.

The phone rang on the main desk, from which I could oversee the counter and the cashiers. I didn't quite hear who the caller was and asked him to repeat his name. The call was from Dover Harbour Passport Control, and the caller asked me to confirm that he was speaking to Malcolm Harris, a senior official at the bank. I wasn't sure how I could help, but he said that he had the West Ham football team with him, as they were travelling across the channel for a match or a training session. They had a problem with one player's passport, the problem being that his passport was still in the hotel. Did I in fact know a gentleman called Tom McAlister, and could I describe him to them? I gave them a vague description of Tom and his Scottish background, confirmed that I knew him to be a goalkeeper with West Ham, and hoped this would help. I suggested that someone at the club would probably be better placed to identify him than I. The call did make me smile that Passport offices would contact a bank to check out a traveller's identity. I also felt a shiver of pride. You can chuckle now!

Many years later I was telling a pal about this experience during a lunch break. We were queueing to pay for a paperback in a well-known bookstore in Sheffield. I had merely mentioned that he was a goalie with Sheffield United when the lady in front of us in the queue turned to me and said inquisitively, "Tom McAlister?" When I nodded affirmatively, she surprised us both when she said, "Used to go out with him back in the day. Lovely fella." Talk about coincidence!

Anyway, back to the plot.

I enjoyed watching Ruth on tele. I had already received a nice signed photo and a long hand-written letter from her, detailing her life so far and her upbringing, so I felt that I knew something about her. I was due to attend the Royal Cornwall Show, looking for photographic work. So would ITV, in the form of Ruth and her team of presenters from Westward.

On the day, BBC Spotlight was giving members of the public, the opportunity to read the news headlines from an autocue, and to then watch themselves back on several screens set up around their mock-up studio. I was tempted to have a go, after all, you never knew who would be secretly watching, some local news producer or similar. Settling back into the presenter's seat, I nervelessly rattled off the news, and waited for the playback. The lady next to me wondered whether she should have a go. Why not I said, I had really enjoyed the experience. Oh, I thought you were one of the professional BBC team presenters, she said, without the slightest hint of sarcasm, and "that's why I asked about having a try". She must have thought I was doing a demonstration. That was good for my ego I can tell you. I was not head hunted though, more's the pity!

I had hesitantly replied to Ruth's letter, and asked her whether she would have any spare time at the show, to perhaps grab a bite to eat or a coffee. Her not-unexpected response, was that she would have very little time to herself, as she was manning the Gus Honeybun roadshow. It should be borne in mind that Gus was a national treasure, a fun little rabbit puppet, renowned for performing bunny-hops to mark children's birthdays, real name Augustus Jeremiah Honeybun. He even had his own theme tune composed by Ed Welch, and presenters such as Fern Britton, Sally Meen and, of course, the lovely Ruth Langsford.

I think I instinctively knew what the response would be, and so, upstaged by a puppet, albeit a famous one at that, I never got to share a coffee with Ruth, otherwise, who knows, that could have been me alongside her on daytime tv instead of Eamonn!

Why, you might ask, didn't I insist on Ruth having 5 minutes, after all, she must have had a break at some point? Why indeed? There was no rival on this occasion that I was aware of – unless you count Gus. Yet, something stopped me making that extra effort. I now believe it may simply have been the fact that, if pursued, pushed, or charmed she may just have said 'Yes'. My lack of self-assurance had let me down. My averageness struck again. It seemed just, and utterly rational to me, that a television presenter should turn little old me down, after all, who did I think I was, approaching someone in the public eye, when I felt certain she would have admirers in higher echelons. I could blame no-one but myself.

14. THE ONE DECISION I MADE TO BETTER MYSELF THAT ACTUALLY WORKED OUT (BUT ONLY FOR A SHORT TIME BEFORE IT TOO TURNED OUT TO BE JUST A PYRRHIC VICTORY!).....................

I don't think anyone can go through life without making at least one decision that appears to have worked out. I say 'appears to have worked out' with good reason.

I was working for the local authority and quietly stagnating. Opportunities for promotion had dried up, I had reached the top of my scale, and prospects of a pay increase were poor. I saw an advert for a job with the Audit Commission, well-paid compared with my current salary, and based in Truro, but on the outskirts of town with free parking. Bonus!

I hadn't applied for a job in years, and only half-heartedly completed the application form, if truth be known, struggling to remember my school exam results. Much to my surprise I got an interview, and with low expectations, I attended on the appointed morning. I felt I didn't do well in the interview, but I was confident I had passed the written test at least.

The Audit Commission was setting up a new team of Housing Benefit experts to check local authorities' subsidy claims, and they were looking for two initial members. I had built up quite a library of knowledge in the 13 years I had worked in housing benefits, and yet I was still shocked to receive a second interview. This time I was more assured. The interviewers seemed much more approachable, and I was comfortable with their questions. Within hours I received confirmation that I had been selected to launch the team, which would work remotely from Cornwall on subsidy claims from authorities at various locations around the country such as North Wales and Sussex. The idea behind the scheme was to reduce the Commission's need for contract staff often employed at excessive rates of pay in the city of London, many with little real experience.

In time, the team grew to 5 strong, with me and my colleague spending hours training the newcomers, before one of the five was appointed to lead the team. Both Dave and I, the original members of the team, went for the job, but were beaten by another of the new recruits, Anna.

It has to be said that we were very successful, achieving all the targets we were set, saving on travel costs, subsistence and wages, and receiving plaudits from the commission hierarchy. Anna was well-liked and she was gaining supporters wherever she went in the organisation.

There was talk of a second team. We were on a real high, when at Christmas we left the office with our targets achieved and confidence soaring.

Then, all of a sudden, and completely out of the blue, the commission had a change of heart. Rather than carry out the audit in the belt and braces way we had been doing, there was to be a simplification of the audit process to allow local practitioners with little or no experience of benefits to perform the checks. Our team would no longer be required and we were given notice. Within 18 months of being set up our fabulously successful team was being disbanded.

Ironic, that having been brave enough to take on the challenge of a new job, circumstances had conspired against me to deny me the benefits of my actions.

Retained on a weekly contract to finish off my commitments, but now relocated in Yorkshire, I began the search for alternative work. My experience with the Commission only served to confirm how sensible I had been not to be tempted to give up steady employment for an unpredictable career in entertainment, whether on stage or in the studio

The 'opening' of Mallyn Studio, with Linda Lusardi. The press photo with the studio owner sidelined by a travel firm and how it should have appeared above. Left, the 'contract'. I learned a lot from the experience.

Open your legs a little wider for me!

In the charts at number 32. The following year the bank gave a prize to the best performing regional candidate

The only picture I have of me at Uni, getting ready for a fancy-dress party as a hippy. Notice Olivia on the poster above my bed!

Just weeks after I produced 1000 post-cards for my home village the post office, having taken 50, changed ownership and all its signage. Another lesson learned and plenty of spare writing material for the house

Now it's photography purely for fun and an annual calendar for family and friends

15. GO ON THEN.......UNI!

It wouldn't be right to ignore my university experience. As you already know, university, in itself, represented a choice. I was not all that keen from the start. After all, it meant leaving the comfort of home and my parents, my (few) real friends, my girlfriend, the green where we all played, my tennis wall, the Co-op where I worked during the summer break, the familiarity of the local towns.

Chosen Hill expected, and that meant a lot of pressure on us all to apply. I applied for universities that would keep me closest to home. I chose colleges that were well-known for their expertise in languages of course, so that I could study subjects I enjoyed, or, should I say, was good at. I picked out Leicester, not far by train, Exeter, on the mainline to the South West, and Cardiff, only just over an hour away. Additionally, I selected Swansea, just down the line from Cardiff, Hull, because of its course, and one other, somewhere in the South East. I received offers from four, and an interview at Leicester, where I showed all my naivety when asked about my favourite French authors. I only really knew the ones we studied at 'A' level, and my answer gave me away. I never got to mention my humorous quip about them having a good football team. One less university to worry about.

Cardiff asked me to achieve a 'B', 'C' and 'D' in my exams, where an 'A' was top mark, and I duly did so, and settled back to make Cardiff my home for 3 years. Swansea rang to offer me a place in spite of my results, and knowing that I had placed them higher on my list of 6 because of the literary fame of Professor Knight, the head of Modern Languages, I accepted the kind offer.

I have already revealed some of my university highlights – the Freshers Week choice of the Badminton Club, the year abroad, my reluctance to join the radio station, my exploits on the football pitch, and the French Society acting.

My first year was to be spent in halls of residence, while I studied English, French and German, before hammering my cause to the mast in year two in the French class. I shared a room with a Cheltenham Grammar School lad called Tim, room 520 in Lewis Jones, handy for its view directly into the girls' hall, and therefore popular with Tim's friends who were all in the RAF cadet scheme. Tim went on to a hugely successful career with the RAF, one of his claims to fame being as captain of the RAF Cresta Run toboggan team.

The first year was tough. Three subjects put quite a strain on a student, physically and mentally. Some couldn't cope with the homesickness and dropped by the wayside. Others found the routine and the 'homework' too demanding and left, or re-sat year one. The odd few enjoyed themselves far too much and therefore decided that university just wasn't for them.

It took its toll.

One of my best friends found refuge in Pinball, which we regularly played outside the campus shop in the Union House. We all loved the challenge of beating our previous best score, but for her the desire to play took over from the need to attend lessons and she tragically turned to theft to supplement her meagre grant income. I recall vividly being interviewed by the police when the theft became public knowledge. It could have had damaging effects upon my career intentions, and it was mainly because I too had been the victim of the theft that the police were able to pinpoint the perpetrator. I had noticed a cheque had been removed from the back of my cheque book and placed a 'stop' on it before it could be cashed. It was a shame, because she was a lovely girl otherwise, and her loss as a dear friend cast a shadow over my second year in Swansea.

A mutual friend of ours, Allan, provided calm and level-headed judgment whenever it was called for. Allan was one of those guys who spoke rarely. He was a quiet, studious type, and, when he did speak, we all took notice.

It was while a group of us were putting the world to rights in his study one day that another shocking event took place.

Tim and his friends in the cadet force regularly visited St Athan for training, after all it was no distance from Swansea, though occasionally he would arrive back at our room late at night or be obliged to stay overnight.

Imagine being a student at uni by day and then add in the pressures of learning to fly at weekends, coupled with the training at St Athan. No wonder that for one unfortunate lad it all became too much.

Simon, not his real name, was smart, tall and good looking. His future with the forces was almost assured. He just had to study hard and keep it together. But depression loomed, and he began to imagine that he was being spied upon, probably by the Russians – we never got the full story – but we understood that he had been reading some very realistic paperback material.

From Allan's room we could see the path and grassy verges that led from Lewis Jones to Union House, and we happened to be gazing out of the window as we chatted away. We could vaguely hear the sound of girls laughing, sniggering really, and, from our right, marching, no, striding along the path towards Union House came young Simon. More sniggering, then pointing, until the whole of Simon came into view. Poor young man, striding along, wearing not a stitch. We were helpless to intervene, and yet we knew it would not end well. We wanted to cry out, but we knew instinctively that it would do no good. There was determination in his steely stare.

Simon made his way into Union House and through to the college on-site Lloyds bank, along the corridor, and into a chair in the barber's to await his turn for a haircut. We later learned that the barber had the foresight to calmly use one of his hairdressing capes to cover the lad's modesty, before summoning the college staff.

The sad thing is that Simon's parents came to take him home without us ever being able to speak to him again, and Tim and his pals never raised the subject for discussion. There was never any consideration that others might have been affected by the events, or offers of stress management. College life simply went on as normal.

The first choice I had to make, was whether to stick to my initial decision to make French my major subject. I thoroughly enjoyed my English classes, but was determined to make a year abroad part of my education, and could have therefore chosen German or French. I seemed to be 'better' at German, certainly from my exam results, but a year in France appealed to me more, and so I made the decision to go with French.

With Sue now a thing of the past, (what a horrible phrase to employ) I started to date. Helen was a Welsh girl from Pembroke Dock, who, like me, was studying modern languages, and we went to the cinema a couple of times. I do remember watching the film version of MASH* with her in '71, but by the time we visited her home town in the summer of my first year at Swansea, we had gone through the hand holding and kissing, and back to hand holding, before the relationship fizzled out. The highlight of our brief relationship, was accompanying Helen to see her hero Cliff Richard in Cardiff. Not that I was a fan, but he shared his show with Marvin, Welch and Farrar and a gorgeous young singer called Olivia Newton-John, whose first record, 'Love Song' I had bought after hearing it on Radio two, and before I clapped eyes on her lovely face. I became one of her biggest fans, purchasing just about every single and album she released in the UK.

Helen, Allan and I also went to see Roxy Music at the Brangwyn Hall on 8 November 1973. I only mention this to allude to my innate ability to judge new talent. In the lead up to the pulsating Roxy Music, with Phil Manzanera sitting to play his guitar, having injured his leg, and Bryan Ferry strutting his stuff to Virginia Plain, a young guy came on as support. He was alone on stage. He was dressed like the conventional Pierrot circus clown, all in white with three big black pom-pom buttons down the front of his costume, his hair flattened beneath a black headscarf, and his voice falsetto and crackly. He sang a couple of numbers, including Giving it all Away, and The Show Must Go On, and I announced my verdict that one thing was certain in this uncertain pop world, that HE would never get anywhere. 3 weeks later, and Leo Sayer was top of the charts.

Helen and I remain good friends to this day, though Helen lives in Germany with her farmer-husband and large family.

As for Olivia Newton-John? I became a huge fan. It is difficult sometimes to realise just how much a fan's life can be affected by his fanaticism. I waited anxiously for every new release, buying singles as soon as they came out, and saving for every album Olivia produced. I estimate that I bought in the region of 20 albums over the years, progressing to compact discs around the early 90s but still loving the decorative album covers. Even though I already had all the songs, I found it impossible not to buy the greatest hit compilations, which offered me an alternative order in which to hear her songs.

I travelled down to London to see ONJ live on stage during her Physical tour, and was disappointed when Labe Siffre satisfied her request from the stage for someone to accompany her on 'You're the One that I Want'. Ten thousand men had joined me in volunteering!

I went to the cinema to see Grease and Xanadu, bought the videos and the dvds, the duets with Cliff Richard and posters to decorate my walls. I scoured the newspapers for news and articles about my Livvy and duly cut them out for my scrapbook. I watched her tv series, and her appearances on Cliff Richard's shows and on Top of the Pops. I recorded an appearance on radio where she spoke passionately about her favourite songs, including a number by Blood Sweat and Tears, and played it back time after time. And above all, I sat with my headphones on, listening to her angelic music, the best live singer I ever heard, note perfect.

Of course, like all men, and many young women too. I found Olivia so very attractive. When I saw her first, I was stunned by her beauty, particularly her gorgeous eyes, and her hair, parted down the middle in a trendy fashion.

I became jealous when I heard about her relationship with Bruce Welch of the Shadows. I was incensed when I found out about her dalliance with Sacha Distel. Less so when Matt Lattanzi came along and married Olivia.

My mum taped and sent me Olivia's 6 Eurovision entry songs for me to hear when I got back to my room at university after attending my lectures. I watched the Song Contest on television in 1974, worried that she would struggle to beat my favourite song, by the eventual winners, Abba. In the event she finished a creditable fourth.

I wrote to Livvy around her birthday each year, sending her a card for 26 September. She sent me autographs, some on my own photos of her album covers.

I shared her successes and her failures, her upsets when friends such as Karen Carpenter and Andy Gibb died far too young, and her struggles with cancer.

Later, in the 2010s, I read her biography. I wondered why in her discography her first single in the UK was quoted as 'If Not For You' and not the one I had bought, 'Love Song'. Both songs were on her first album.

xxxxxxxxxxxxxxxxxxxxxxxxxxxxxxxxxxxxxxxxxxxxxxxxxxxxxxxxxxxxxxx

In the second year, I discovered that one of the pretty waitresses in the college canteen was handing me extra-large portions with a winning smile, and before too long we were dating. Most of the lads fancied her, but I bravely stepped up to the counter and asked her out for a drink. Vivienne hailed from Newcastle, and she had just the one bad habit – she smoked! Though she promised to give them up, she would occasionally sneak a crafty fag during the night, and dispose of the butt out of the window, forgetting maybe that smoke does tend to linger in the air, and leaves tell-tale stains on clothes and fingers.

In spite of this, we spent a lot of time together. Viv was even with me in my room, when dad turned up early to run me home at the end of term. Bedrooms in the hall of residence were just that: they had a bed, a wardrobe, a 'comfy' chair and a desk and study chair. There was hardly anywhere to sit together. Someone always seemed to have to perch on the bed, so when dad turned up Viv and I were naturally sat on the bed together, chatting while we packed the last of my belongings in my case for the journey home. He did not look amused at the time, but I have to say that both my parents came to think highly of her once they got to know her and her considerate ways better.

Neither did the apparent gap in our intellects cause any difficulties. Viv had left school at 16, and worked straight away in the service industry. No 'A' levels for her. We got on like a house on fire, though I always seemed to be in teacher-pupil mode with Viv, a situation which she fully accepted and even enjoyed. I always felt that she was capable of being so much more in life than catering to the likes of me and my fellow students. I wanted our relationship to last, in spite of our differences, because Viv and I were simply good for one another, and I was at that age, when you start thinking long term and are desperate to meet that certain someone. Deep down however, I realised that Viv, as attractive and charming as she was, never was going to be my life-partner.

I needn't have worried because, once again, distance put a swift end to the relationship while I was in France, and by the time my year abroad came to a close in the summer of '73, Viv had got engaged. Letters home could never be a substitute for my fabulous personality of course, and added to this, I was away for 6 months without returning to England, spending Christmas abroad, much to mother's irritation.

There were times when university afforded us enjoyment that the 'outside world' was incapable of doing. In the spring of my first year at Swansea, the band playing in the round on the occasion of our Valentine's Ball, was an outfit who, the year I had left school, had been number one with 'In The Summertime'; Mungo Jerry. The dance hall was warm, going on hot, and full of enthusiastic young revellers. The band were giving it their all, and at the intermission the lead singer made for the bar and passed close by me. Ray Dorset was perhaps best known for his distinctive sideburns, and in person he looked no different. I reached out a hand to pat him on the shoulder, which glistened back at me in the harsh disco lights. My palm slipped as it met with a pool of perspiration.

On 22 February 1972, we wandered down the path into Union House, on our way to dinner in the adjoining College House. Dinner was a formal enough event, same time, same place, same table, and we usually strolled down to the building a few minutes early to establish our usual seats. Occasionally there was a chance that if your table was lacking in numbers, they would split you up and ask you to relocate on another incomplete table, and we weren't keen on that.

As we approached the entrance to the building, we began to notice small hand-written notices which advertised a concert later that night. It read, mysteriously, "Playing tonight, Paul McCartney, Debates Chamber, 10pm: 50p".

This notice caused a bit of a debate in itself. First of all, was this the real Paul McCartney, the ex-Beatle we had so long admired? Even true Beatles fans argued that it was unlikely to be right. The price of 50p seemed unreal too. Any former Beatle would surely demand a ticket price far in excess of 50 pence? And as locations for live music went, the debates chamber was not the first one that would spring to mind for its fine acoustics. By and large then, we dismissed the notice as a student prank.

By 8 o'clock, a small but determined queue had formed beneath Union House where the debates Chamber was located. Our route back from dinner took us past the queue, and we could not help thinking that the prank had gone too far. Even when at 10 o'clock the queue had grown substantially, there was no sign of Paul or indeed any equipment. And then at around 10.30 there was movement. The queue started to edge forward. I could see all this from my room on campus. One or two of us who had seen the notice decided to gather outside on the grass, the same grass where young Simon had caused such a sensation the year before.

To explain, the debates chamber was on the side of Union House that overlooked Singleton Park, and between Union House and Singleton Park the ground rose significantly, which meant that tight-fisted students who found 50 pence expensive, or who could not be assed to queue for things that may or may not actually come to fruition, could stand on the grass at almost the same level as the debates chamber, and look straight in. Word was now spreading, that Paul and his new band, Wings, had arrived in Swansea late from Birmingham, dropped their gear, and gone off to search for a bed and breakfast for the night, before returning to play. Within minutes, instruments were being tuned.

This would in fact be the first time Wings had played a venue outside England, and when the band struck up, we had the perfect view. They played a few classic rock numbers, 'Long Tall Sally' being one of them. We could hear McCartney's characteristic falsetto voice and his bass guitar through the windows, now open to prevent them from steaming up.

After a few more songs our free concert came abruptly to an end, as the audience indoors realised that we were gathered outside. Windows were closed, and the blinds were pulled to obscure our view. Some of us had the cheek to boo.

We hung around long enough to say 'we were there' before trudging back to our rooms. Ironically, we could hear better through our own open windows higher up the slope. History had been made, and we had been a part of it. So much for the doubters. I knew he would turn up, of course!

Another band that played at uni, was intriguingly a French group called Ange, or, simple translation, angel. They were a progressive rock band in the style of Red Crimson, and, some- time later, they opened for Genesis at the Reading Festival of 1973. They sang exclusively in French, otherwise the Decamps brothers would undoubtedly have been more successful on the British scene.

The final year at university was a rigorous one. I was never going to get a First. Very few people did, and those were the exceptional candidates, those who were not only gifted but who worked their socks off and deserved everything they got.

I hated the library with its enforced silence and its diligence. I preferred to work in my room, so would do some preparation in the library, checking with the giant Larousse dictionaries or text books, before writing up my essays or translations back at my desk where I could half listen to my music as I worked, sometimes well into the night to meet deadlines. I still carried the burden of the 'home for tea' essay perception, which limited the length and extent of my written work and therefore my marks too. Yes, I was never in line for a first degree. The level of my grade 2 Honours degree would depend on my own level of commitment.

With much time in my final year spent chasing an Olivia Newton-John lookalike, following her around college, visiting her room, while she worked away to the background sounds of Ralph McTell, or completely ignored me while I sat on the bed, taking her to the on-site cinema or the union bar, I guess I was establishing my rights to the 2 (ii) I was inevitably heading for. If I had put as much effort into my studies as I did in pursuing my perfect girl, I could maybe have achieved that elusive 2 (i), but one task was considerably easier than the other, and so much more pleasurable, though ultimately totally fruitless. Yet another friend for life, I am glad to say.

Towards the end of the final year, the university invited students to meet and greet representatives of various well-known employers, with a view to choosing a career. Having spent a year in France I was not seeking to return there for work, and once more the words of my father ran through my head. His influence was significant, not for the first time, and, thinking about it now, probably not the last. Old-school in his attitude to life, my father praised the concept of a secure employment, a career for life, and, therefore, was instrumental in my decision to seek a career in either banking or insurance, in spite of considering both as potentially boring and lacking creativity.

In the event, I found myself drawn to finance, and applied for half a dozen jobs in each of the two service industries. They all advertised graduate programmes which would accelerate my progress through to middle management, and this did sound attractive, together with a decent salary and long-term prospects. Banks were still opening branches in the 70s and insurance was going through a boom period, so I felt confident in my choices vis-à-vis dad's parameters.

I rejected careers with higher wages but more risk, and avoided jobs where degrees made little difference to progression. Surely, I was following the right route, the safe route, the logical route?

Allan had thought about teaching at a girls' school in Cardiff, or a librarianship, but in the end, he plumped for a further course in translation in London, before applying for and obtaining work in the European Parliament in Luxembourg. We are still in touch. Allan has lived on the Continent ever since and now resides in Brussels.

Tim pursued his RAF career, while Helen went on to live in Germany. My choice seemed dull and mundane by comparison.

I had clearly not yet learned to make decisions for myself. Parental influence was still overwhelming. My mother would have been happy for me to 'get a little job in Cheltenham' so that I could continue living at home. And in spite of dad's own personal commitment at an early age to join the forces and 'see the world', his ambitions for me had been less expansive, and for my sins, I had simply surrendered to his well-meaning suggestions.

Another of dad's ideas was that I should apply for the civil service at GCHQ. A friend of his, had a son who had started work there after his 'A' levels, and with my foreign language degree, I would be a prime candidate, he believed. Purely coincidentally, of course, GCHQ happened to be in Cheltenham, and thus satisfied mum's red lines too.

I couldn't see, or I possibly hid from the fact, that my life was being governed by my father. No surprise then, that I found the world of banking physical, repetitive and difficult to grasp, no real mental test, and yet full of rules and regulations, which all needed learning at night school over the next three years.

I finished the exams as top Midland Bank employee in the South West of England, cementing my place in the world's top 50 candidates completing their banking exams in September '78. The following year the bank introduced a prize for the highest achiever in these self-same exams, and, had it come in the previous year, I would have been the recipient. Was this yet another example of my averageness?

EPILOGUE

Back in school, when I was just a child, the teacher would set a rough target of words to complete an essay, or a composition as it was then known. "Listen everyone, try and do 300 words!"

I would count up every two or so lines of writing, noting the number in pencil in the margin. When I was approaching the target, say 10% off, I would start to draw the story to a close. After all, no point in wasting good footballing time, and the other kids had been out on the green for hours now. Yes, it was getting dark, but we could carry on under the street lights for ages yet. 295, 296, 297, add an adjective or two here and there, 298, 299 and they all went home for tea. Done.

Now, as I write, I feel no pressure. No time constraints. No football to get to, no goals to score while we can still just about make out the damp jumpers on the soggy grass. No, just a time to stop and think, to take it all in, to contemplate.

What has it all been about?

Where has that little boy gone, the genius? Well, he isn't here anymore. In his place is an old man. An average old man with a story to tell.

Once upon a time there was a little boy. He was shy, but he was bright. His star shone brightest at home, where he was safe and secure, where he could do no wrong. School became an extension of home. More brilliance. Praised to the gunnels by teachers, prizes at year-end, never seen the like. Still painfully shy, but now so nonchalant about his own ability.

Imagine this young boy, with his high IQ, leaving junior school and heading for grammar school, one of just four from his school to pass the 11 plus. You would imagine his confidence would be sky high based on his infant school experiences, but remember, this lad had no siblings, few friends, no pal to travel to school with.

It wasn't immediate, but ever so gradually there was a realisation that many more stars existed in the universe than just our Malcolm, and that his was far from being the brightest. It is easy to see how this growing recognition must have negatively impacted upon our eleven-year-old. No longer the apple of teacher's eye. Struggling to get good marks, or at least top scores, where previously it had been oh so easy.

Little surprise then that our child genius suffered from a deflated sense of importance. This nervous, solitary youngster retreated further into his shell.

And although there had, genuinely, been a drop in his level of achievement, it was never as severe or decisive as he perceived it to be. In his mind he had fallen from the summit to somewhere near the foot of the mountain, whereas in reality he was clinging on to a ledge, feet from the top.

He only had his parents to relate to. All his pals attended the local secondary. They were far from interested in trying to analyse his circumstances. Teachers in those days were untrained in psychology and too busy to concern themselves about how individual kids were feeling 'in themselves'. Provided the children turned up and seemed relatively untroubled. On the face of it, Malcolm was not doing as well as his junior school career had predicted, and his form teacher said just that. At fourteenth in class he had slipped 13 places, and yet in reality he was still 107 spots clear of bottom position in his year. At grammar school. With university in his sights. And all he could think of was how 'average' he was.

I have read and re-read this book over and over in the writing and editing process. You would imagine that I would be wiser for the experience, that I would now be able to decipher the decisions I have made.

But you know, I am none the wiser, just older.

Next up, a classic from the Beatles, but first, with a new release, Mal Harris, and the title track from his forthcoming album, A Mere Mortal, here on Vital FM.

Printed in Poland
by Amazon Fulfillment
Poland Sp. z o.o., Wrocław